Foreign Direct Investment and Strategic Alliances in Europe

Foreign Direct Investment and Strategic Alliances in Europe has been co-published simultaneously as *Journal of Euromarketing*, Volume 10, Number 1 2001.

The *Journal of Euromarketing* Monographic "Separates"

Below is a list of "separates," which in serials librarianship means a special issue simultaneously published as a special journal issue or double-issue *and* as a "separate" hardbound monograph. (This is a format which we also call a "DocuSerial.")

"Separates" are published because specialized libraries or professionals may wish to purchase a specific thematic issue by itself in a format which can be separately cataloged and shelved, as opposed to purchasing the journal on an on-going basis. Faculty members may also more easily consider a "separate" for classroom adoption.

"Separates" are carefully classified separately with the major book jobbers so that the journal tie-in can be noted on new book order slips to avoid duplicate purchasing.

You may wish to visit Haworth's website at . . .

http://www.HaworthPress.com

. . . to search our online catalog for complete tables of contents of these separates and related publications.

You may also call 1-800-HAWORTH (outside US/Canada: 607-722-5857), or Fax: 1-800-895-0582 (outside US/Canada: 607-771-0012), or e-mail at:

getinfo@haworthpressinc.com

Foreign Direct Investment and Strategic Alliances in Europe, edited by Hong Liu, PhD (Vol. 10, No. 1, 2001). *Foreign direct investment (FDI) and strategic alliances are among the most popular modes of international market entry and expansion in major markets by multinationals. This book integrates FDI issues with those of strategic alliances to deliver insights into both areas and provides up-close perspectives on specific segments of the European market. It uses case studies, a wide-ranging survey, and the expertise of authorities in the field to shed light on the* when, why, *and* how *of investing and forming alliances in the volatile environment of the European market.*

Global Marketing Co-Operation and Networks, edited by Leo Paul Dana, BA, MBA, PhD (Vol. 9, No. 2, 2000). *"Excellent . . . . well-referenced . . . . very useful. I for one have found it to be current, effective, and useful for developing my own research and teaching materials." (Claudio Vignali, BA, MPhil, DipM, Senior Lecturer, Manchester Metropolitan University, United Kingdom)*

Cross-National Consumer Psychographics, edited by Lynn R. Kahle (Vol. 8, No. 1/2, 1999). "Cross-National Consumer Psychographics *provides marketing professionals and students with data from several applications around the world of the list of values (LOV), so you can consider the implications for understanding consumers cross-culturally. Through this unique book you will find how different countries and different individual consumers may be segmented based on their social values so you can develop the best marketing strategies for your products."*

Newer Insights into Marketing: Cross-Cultural and Cross-National Perspectives, edited by Camille P. Schuster, PhD, and Phil Harris, BA (Hons) (Vol. 7, No. 2, 1999). *This new book analyzes and investigates international marketing strategies to determine effective marketing practices of businesses in the global arena.*

Green Marketing in a Unified Europe, edited by Alma T. Mintu-Wimsatt, PhD, and Héctor R. Lozada, PhD (Vol. 5, No. 3, 1996). "Takes a well-researched and heartfelt approach to the 3 P's of environmental marketing–preservation, protection, and proactive product development." (Debbie Thorne, PhD, Director, Center for Ethics, The University of Tampa)

International Joint Ventures in East Asia, edited by Roger Baran, PhD, Yigang Pan, PhD, and Erdener Kaynak, PhD, DSc (Vol. 4, No. 3/4, 1996). "A valuable resource for anyone interested in joint ventures anywhere in the world." (Sunder Narayanan, PhD, Assistant Professor, School of Business, Columbia University)

Ethical Issues in International Marketing, edited by Nejdet Delener, PhD (Vol. 4, No. 2, 1995). "Provides an invaluable education to the reader and encourages the reader to think about important issues that increasingly confront businesspeople in their dealings within a global marketplace." (George V. Priovolos, PhD, CPA, Assistant Professor, Marketing Department, Hagan School of Business, Iona College)

The Impact of Innovation and Technology in the Global Marketplace, edited by Shaker A. Zahra, PhD, and Abbas J. Ali, PhD (Vol. 3, No. 3/4, 1994). "The editors have captured the excitement of the present day technological innovations with a wise selection of scholarly articles. Grab this book and read it before it's too late!" (Raymond A. K. Cox, PhD, Professor of Finance, Central Michigan University)

Foreign Direct Investment and Strategic Alliances in Europe

Hong Liu, PhD
Editor

Foreign Direct Investment and Strategic Alliances in Europe has been co-published simultaneously as *Journal of Euromarketing*, Volume 10, Number 1 2001.

Routledge
Taylor & Francis Group
LONDON AND NEW YORK

Foreign Direct Investment and Strategic Alliances in Europe **has been co-published simultaneously as** ***Journal of Euromarketing*****, Volume 10, Number 1 2001.**

First published 2001 by The Haworth Press, Inc.

2 Park Square, Milton Park, Abingdon, Oxfordshire OX14 4RN
605 Third Avenue, New York, NY 10017

Routledge is an imprint of the Taylor & Francis Group, an informa business

First issued in hardback 2020

Cover design by Thomas J. Mayshock Jr.

Library of Congress Cataloging-in-Publication Data

Foreign direct investment and strategic alliances in Europe/Hong Liu, editor.
p. cm.
"Co-published simultaneously as Journal of Euromarketing, volume 10, number 1, 2001."
Inclues bibliographical references and index.
ISBN 0-7890-1652-4 (alk. paper)–ISBN 0-7890-1653-2 (alk. paper)
1. Investments, Foreign–Europe. 2. International business enterprises–Europe. I. Liu, Hong.
HG5422.F669 2001
332.67'314'094–dc21 2001039485

ISBN 978-0-7890-1652-2 (hbk)

∞ ALL INTERNATIONAL BUSINESS PRESS BOOKS AND JOURNALS ARE PRINTED ON CERTIFIED ACID-FREE PAPER

Indexing, Abstracting & Website/Internet Coverage

This section provides you with a list of major indexing & abstracting services. That is to say, each service began covering this periodical during the year noted in the right column. Most Websites which are listed below have indicated that they will either post, disseminate, compile, archive, cite or alert their own Website users with research-based content from this work. (This list is as current as the copyright date of this publication.)

Abstracting, Website/Indexing Coverage	Year When Coverage Began
• *Anbar Management Intelligence Abstracts*	2000
• *BUBL Information Service, an Internet-based Information Service for the UK higher education community <URL: http://bubl.ac.uk/>*	1996
• *CNPIEC Reference Guide: Chinese National Directory of Foreign Periodicals*	1996
• *Contents of this publication are indexed and abstracted in the ABI/INFORM database, available on Bell & Howell Information & Learning's ProQuest @www.umi.com*	1992
• *FINDEX <www.publist.com>*	1999
• *Foods Adlibra*	1991
• *GEO Abstracts (GEO Abstracts/GEOBASE) <URL: http://www.elsevier.nl>*	1993
• *Human Resources Abstracts (HRA)*	1991

(continued)

- ***Index Guide to College Journals (core list compiled by integrating 48 indexes frequently used to support undergraduate programs in small to medium sized libraries)*** **1999**
- ***Management & Marketing Abstracts*** **1991**
- ***Market Research Abstracts*** **1996**
- ***Marketing & Distribution Abstracts*** **1997**
- ***Operations Research/Management Science*** **1992**
- ***Sage Public Administration Abstracts (SPAA)*** **1991**
- ***Sage Urban Studies Abstracts (SUSA)*** **1991**
- ***Sociological Abstracts (SA) <www.csa.com>*** **1992**

Special Bibliographic Notes related to special journal issues (separates) and indexing/abstracting:

- indexing/abstracting services in this list will also cover material in any ''separate'' that is co-published simultaneously with Haworth's special thematic journal issue or DocuSerial. Indexing/abstracting usually covers material at the article/chapter level.
- monographic co-editions are intended for either non-subscribers or libraries which intend to purchase a second copy for their circulating collections.
- monographic co-editions are reported to all jobbers/wholesalers/approval plans. The source journal is listed as the ''series'' to assist the prevention of duplicate purchasing in the same manner utilized for books-in-series.
- to facilitate user/access services all indexing/abstracting services are encouraged to utilize the co-indexing entry note indicated at the bottom of the first page of each article/chapter/contribution.
- this is intended to assist a library user of any reference tool (whether print, electronic, online, or CD-ROM) to locate the monographic version if the library has purchased this version but not a subscription to the source journal.
- individual articles/chapters in any Haworth publication are also available through the Haworth Document Delivery Service (HDDS).

Foreign Direct Investment and Strategic Alliances in Europe

CONTENTS

ABOUT THE EDITOR

Hong Liu, PhD, joined the Manchester Business School in 1992 with a background in engineering and economics. He completed his PhD in marketing at Warwick Business School, having been awarded a Hong Kong Marketing scholarship. As a frequent speaker to both multinational companies and Chinese officials and enterprises, he acted as a consultant for the OECD, the Brunei government, the Chinese government, and a number of major multinationals. Dr. Liu is Director of the China Business Centre at the Manchester Business School and has been awarded a number of grants from the British government and United Nations for research and management training. He worked with scholars from North America, Europe, and Japan on business strategies for European integration in two collaborative projects. He has published numerous papers in international journals as well as book chapters on international marketing and marketing strategies.

Introduction

Although American multinationals have had a strong presence in Europe after World War II, Europe has experienced a steady increase in the inflow of foreign direct investment FDI from American, Japanese, and, more recently, Korean companies since the mid-1980s. About half of US firms' FDI took place in Europe, with the UK being the leader as the destination for FDI. Other major FDI recipients include Ireland, France, Germany and the Netherlands. The same period has also witnessed a dramatic rise in the formation of strategic alliances among the firms of Triad countries of Europe, North America, and Asia.

Lorange and Roos (1993, p. 3) have defined strategic alliances as ventures along a continuous scale from a high to low degree of vertical integration. FDI (acquisition, greenfield investment and equity joint ventures) may be seen as on the side of a high degree of vertical integration while strategic alliances are on the side of a low degree of vertical integration, with joint ventures shared by both. FDI and strategic alliances are among the most popular modes of international market entry and expansion in major markets by multinationals. Figure 1 presents a framework for FDI and strategic alliances in Europe in terms of the geographic scope (Western versus Eastern and Central Europe), environmental conditions, and strategic motives.

Doing business in Western Europe is a completely different ballgame from that in Eastern and Central Europe. Western Europe presents the largest market in the world, has a stable business environment and offers an excellent technology or knowledge base. At the same time, competition there is cut-throat and entry barriers are relatively high. American, Japanese, and Korean firms engaging in FDI and strategic

---

[Haworth co-indexing entry note]: "Introduction." Liu, Hong. Co-published simultaneously in *Journal of Euromarketing* (International Business Press, an imprint of The Haworth Press, Inc.) Vol. 10, No. 1, 2001, pp. 1-4; and: *Foreign Direct Investment and Strategic Alliances in Europe* (ed: Hong Liu) International Business Press, an imprint of The Haworth Press, Inc., 2001, pp. 1-4. Single or multiple copies of this article are available for a fee from The Haworth Document Delivery Service [1-800-342-9678, 9:00 a.m. - 5:00 p.m. (EST). E-mail address: getinfo@haworthpressinc.com].

FIGURE 1. A Framework for FDI and Strategic Alliances in Europe

	Strategic Motives	Environmental Conditions
Eastern and Central European Countries	• Production location/base • Market development • Legal/regulatory considerations • First mover advantage	• Low labour cost • New markets/less competition • Inadequate infrastructure • Underdeveloped legal system • Investment incentives
	Strategic Motives	Environmental Conditions
Western European Countries	• "Single European Market" push • Market development/expansion • Technology/resource acquisition • Risk sharing • Pursuit of global strategy	• Cut-throat competition • Knowledge/technology base • Stable environment • Sizable markets • High entry barriers
Foreign Direct Investment		Strategic Alliances
Acquisition Greenfield Investment	Joint Ventures	Formal/Informal Co-operative Agreement

alliances in Western Europe are mainly motivated by the Single European Market Program, market development or expansion, the pursuit of global strategies, technology/knowledge and resource acquisition and risk sharing. General Motors has recently formed a strategic alliance with Fiat, as part of GM's strategy to become a global car maker, in order to secure cooperation in the automotive markets of both Europe and Latin America. In forming a strategic alliance between Mitsubishi and Volvo, the Japanese partner believes that the alliance would help the firm gain competitiveness in an increasingly competitive international marketplace while the Volvo management expects the partnership to open up possibilities for further cooperation between the two companies. Having acquired 95 stores in Germany, Wal-Mart, the American retail giant, has triggered a wave of mergers and acquisitions in the European retail sector. Germany was chosen because it provides a central springboard for the American company to expand further into the Continent, and Wal-Mart's customer-focused culture seems to have gained an edge in the German retail sector where customer services have been lacking.

Since 1989 there has been a rapid increase in FDI and strategic alliances (joint ventures) in many Eastern and Central European countries as a result of the changes in their political and economic environment. Because of a short period of decentralization in these countries, the business environment has still left much to be desired. Legal systems and marketing infrastructure still need to be developed further. For instance, recently Pernod Ricard, a French drinks group, has experienced some difficulties in Poland as a result of legislative flaws. Having bought one of the largest Polish food firms to acquire the firm's franchise to sell such lucrative popular vodka brands as Wyborowa, Pernod only later found that it could be stripped of the right to sell the brand (*The Economist* 2000). Because of the nature of the business environment, strategic motives and the mode of market entry are context specific. The reasons for a Western firm entering a joint venture may relate to legal requirements or to a consideration for risk sharing.

This volume including five papers covers a wide range of issues on FDI and strategic alliances in Western and Eastern Europe. The first paper authored by Tamar Almor examines the relationship between contextual and strategic factors and foreign market entry strategies in the context in which Israeli manufacturers developed their entry strategies in the European Union. The paper points to the direction of a contingency view of market entry strategies based on a multivariate model. The paper by Robert E. Morgan and Eleri R. Thorpe addresses some underlying FDI episodes of multinationals in transition economies. Using a case study approach, it discusses the Coca-Cola company in Russia in terms of its market entry, development and expansion, strategic problems and barriers to expansion, and first- versus late-mover advantages in this transition economy. The paper offers insights into strategic development for firms that operate in, or will enter, Eastern and Central Europe.

Rod McNaughton focuses on US software firms in their relationships with European firms in terms of the choice between market entry modes and characteristics such as the host country, industrial sector, range of functions covered by the relationship, and technological intensity or year in which the relationship occurred. The framework and findings in the paper provide practitioners with some guidelines on several broad influences on the choice of alliance form. In their paper, Saleema Kauser and Vivienne Shaw present a survey of 114 international strategic alliances between UK firms and their European, US and Japanese partners concerning the influence of behavioral characteristics on the success of international strategic alliances. The study suggests that high levels of co-ordination, commitment, trust and communications have a positive impact on international partnership success, and conflict can hinder a good performance. Richard Schoenberg's paper examines a special issue on acquisitions–the types of knowledge transfer and resource sharing sought by inbound European acquirers together with their relative success rates. His study indicates that cross-border acquirers consistently underestimate the difficulty in implementing planned operational synergies and explains insightfully why inbound European. acquisitions continue to generate disappointing shareholder returns.

FDI and strategic alliances are expected to continue to flourish in Europe. By integrating issues of FDI with those of strategic alliances, I hope this special edition will inspire further research into the "integrative issues" and provide both students of international business and practitioners with insights into general issues on FDI and strategic alliances as well as unique perspectives on Europe.

Hong Liu

REFERENCES

Peter Lorange & Johan Roos (1993), Strategic Alliances: Formation, Implementation, and Evolution, Blackwell Publishers.

The Economist (2000), "Business: On the rocks," The Economist, August 26, 52-53.

Towards a Contingency View of Market Entry Strategies: Contextual and Strategic Factors

Tamar Almor

SUMMARY. The model presented in this paper examines the relationship between contextual and strategic factors and foreign market entry strategies in the form of: (1) wholly-owned marketing subsidiaries, (2) international joint ventures, (3) international strategic alliances, (4) exports.

Hypotheses are presented and tested on a sample of Israeli manufacturers who market their products in the European Union. Results show that each entry mode has a different contextual and strategic configuration, thus supporting the need for a contingency view. *[Article copies available for a fee from The Haworth Document Delivery Service: 1-800-342-9678. E-mail address: <getinfo@haworthpressinc.com> Website: <http://www.HaworthPress.com> © 2001 by The Haworth Press, Inc. All rights reserved.]*

KEYWORDS. Market entry strategies, FDI, international strategic alliances, international joint ventures, export, contingency view of entry modes

---

Tamar Almor is Senior Lecturer and Head of Management and Organization and Integrative Studies, College of Management–Academic Studies, School of Business Administration, 7 Itzak Rabin Blvd, P.O.B. 9017, 75190 Rishon LeZion, Israel (E-mail: talmor@colman.ac.il).

The author wishes to thank the Research Unit of the College of Management–Academic Studies for its financial support of an earlier version of this paper.

[Haworth co-indexing entry note]: "Towards a Contingency View of Market Entry Strategies: Contextual and Strategic Factors." Almor, Tamar. Co-published simultaneously in *Journal of Euromarketing* (International Business Press, an imprint of The Haworth Press, Inc.) Vol. 10, No. 1, 2001, pp. 5-25; and: *Foreign Direct Investment and Strategic Alliances in Europe* (ed: Hong Liu) International Business Press, an imprint of The Haworth Press, Inc., 2001, pp. 5-25. Single or multiple copies of this article are available for a fee from The Haworth Document Delivery Service [1-800-342-9678, 9:00 a.m. - 5:00 p.m. (EST). E-mail address: getinfo@haworthpressinc.com].

INTRODUCTION

Research regarding choice of market entry mode has largely focused on contextual variables such as country of origin and industry (e.g., Almor & Hirsch, 1995; Braunerhjelm & Oxelheim, 1992; Chang and Rosenzweig, 1998; Nitsch, Beamish and Makino, 1996; Oxelheim & Gärtner, 1996), size (e.g., Agarwal & Ramashwami, 1992; Buckley and Casson, 1976; Calof, 1994) and ownership (e.g., Argarwal and Ramaswami, 1992; Kogut and Singh, 1988). Other researchers have studied strategic variables in relation to market entry strategies such as a firm's strategy, knowledge transfer and its perception of the competitive environment (e.g., Anderson and Gatignon, 1986; Calof & Beamish, 1995; Caves and Mehra, 1986; Gatignon and Anderson, 1988; Kim and Hwang, 1992; Kogut and Singh, 1988; Kogut and Zander, 1993). The various studies show that contextual as well as strategic variables are related to choice of market entry strategies.

Entry mode choice is contingent upon variables such as size, industry and ownership on one hand, but is also shaped by perceptions of the market the firm wants to enter, its dependence upon that market, and the firm's international experience. Indeed, Calof and Beamish (1995) argue that choice of market entry strategy is a complex phenomenon that can only be explained by examining various factors simultaneously. This paper attempts to explain choice of market entry strategies in terms of strategic as well as contextual considerations, while comparing four different market entry modes: wholly-owned sales subsidiaries (WOS), international joint ventures (IJV), international strategic alliances (ISA) and export.

The four market entry strategies are situated on a continuum that can be perceived in terms of control; the higher the degree of foreign direct investment (FDI), the higher the firm's control over it's foreign markets. Various researchers have discussed the importance of control over resources in order to succeed in a foreign market (Anderson and Gatignon, 1986; Kim and Hwang, 1992; Kogut and Zander, 1993). Comparison of the four market entry strategies in relation to contextual and strategic variables will enable us to understand what makes firms relinquish control and under which conditions.

The contextual factor is comprised of three variables and includes type of industry, type of ownership and size. The strategic factor includes international experience, dependence upon foreign markets and perception of the foreign market in terms of uncertainty, change and opportunities. The model studied here is presented in Figure 1. A short discussion of the variables in the model follows

INTERNATIONAL MARKET ENTRY STRATEGIES

Wholly-owned subsidiaries are based on foreign direct investment (FDI). FDI theory has been developed since the early 1960s (Hymer, 1976) and finds its basis in international trade theory and the industrial organization approach (Karlsen, 1991). Firms employ FDI because of ownership advantages or firm-specific advantages. Since exploitation

FIGURE 1. Contextual and Strategic Factors Related to Choice of Entry Mode

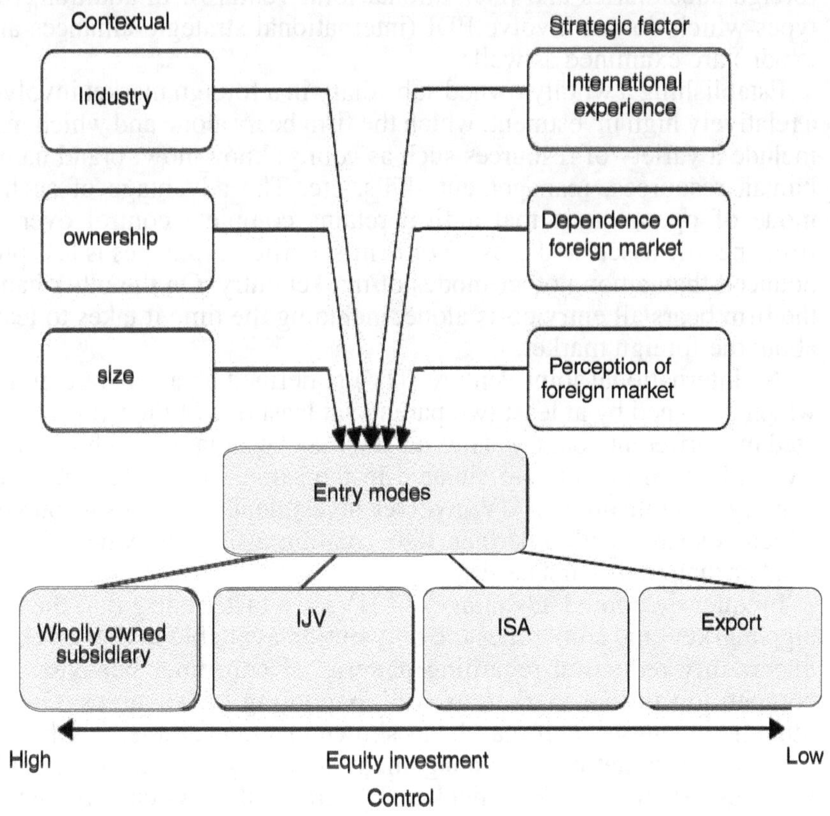

of firm-specific assets may be eroded through arm's-length trade, firms tend to internalize assets by establishing foreign subsidiaries (Caves, 1982; Dunning, 1981, 1988; Heum & Ylä-Anttila, 1993). Firm specific advantages in combination with market imperfections enable a firm operating in a foreign market to enlarge its profits through FDI.

Empirical research on FDI by firms from different countries has been prolific (e.g., Almor & Hirsch, 1995; Bellak, 1996; Braunerhjelm & Oxelheim, 1992; Heum & Ylä-Anttila, 1993; Kojima, 1990; Kojima and Ozawa, 1984; Oxelheim & Gärtner, 1996). However, most of these studies look at macro economic trends and industry differences and do not address variables at the firm level. Moreover, most studies assume full ownership of the foreign subsidiaries. In this study we look at two types of market entry modes which are based on FDI: wholly-owned foreign subsidiaries and international joint ventures. In addition, two types which do not involve FDI (international strategic alliances and export) are examined as well.

Establishing a wholly owned subsidiary in a foreign market involves a relatively high investment, which the firm bears alone and which may include a variety of resources such as equity, know-how, brand name, human resources, management skills, etc. The advantage of such a mode of operation is that a firm retains complete control over its firm-specific assets and erosion of firm-specific advantages is less pronounced than among other modes of market entry. On the other hand, the firm bears all entry costs alone, including the time it takes to learn about the foreign market.

An international joint venture (IJV) is defined as a separate entity, which is owned by at least two parents; at least one of the firms is situated in a different country. Thus an IJV may be situated in a host country while both parents are situated in the same, or a different, home country. Establishing an IJV involves investment of various resources, which is shared with a partner, thus creating a situation where FDI is smaller than in the first case.

Frequently quoted advantages of IJVs are faster entry into the foreign market (and sometimes the only option available in that market), uncertainty reduction regarding patterns of consumer behavior and competition in that market, as well as pooling of resources. On the other hand, empirical research has shown that management of the IJV is more problematic than management of wholly owned foreign subsidiaries (Shenkar, 1990; Shenkar & Zeira, 1987). As each partner is part owner of the IJV, it retains partial control of its own firm-specific advantages as well as over the new advantages created, however, this control is less pronounced than in the case of WOS and may be problematic.

International strategic alliances (ISAs), different forms of cooperation or hybrids as they are called as well, are defined in various ways. Nevertheless, most researchers agree that strategic alliances are bilateral, or sometimes multilateral, arrangements between firms which exist for a certain purpose and period of time (i.e., Borys & Jemison, 1989; Jarillo, 1988; Porter & Fuller, 1986; Powell, 1987). ISAs are defined in this paper as long term cooperation agreements with a foreign firm which are not based on equity, but rather on intangible resources such as know-how, brand name, market and technical knowledge, managerial skills, etc. Thus, they involve investment of resources, but not FDI and, consequently, they rate low on control over firm-specific advantages. The difference between ISAs and IJVs lies in the fact that firms using ISAs do not establish a subsidiary, but rather use existing facilities (of the local partner) to operate in the host country.

ISAs allow relatively small firms to enter the international market by pooling tangible and intangible resources, thereby forming a *virtual* larger company (e.g., Bleeke & Ernst, 1993; Ohmae, 1989; Porter & Fuller, 1986; Powell, 1987). ISAs also allow firms to create joint competitive advantages (Hamel et al., 1988; Ohmae, 1989), enter new markets, overcome high entrance barriers and deal with environmental uncertainty (Powell, 1987). However, ISAs are notoriously unstable (Bery & Bowers, 1993; Bleeke & Ernst, 1993) and are mainly based on trust and cooperation, thus allowing for relatively low levels of control over firm-specific advantages.

One argument brought forward frequently regarding the choice of ISA as a market entry strategy is that it allows firms to deal with uncertainty. Ohmae (1989) argues that in a changeable world of rapidly globalizing markets and industries, firms do not have a choice but to experiment with ISAs. Researchers such as Hergert and Morris (1988), Porter and Fuller (1986) and Pucik (1988) argue that firms operating in an unpredictable environment where variance of return is very large, will prefer to share the risk rather than to go it alone. Powell (1987) proposes that when the environment is very dynamic, firms will prefer alliances as a way to reposition themselves quickly without incurring the high costs associated with internalization and without loss of flexibility. Summarizing, it is clear that perception of the environment in terms of uncertainty or change plays an important role in the explanation of the existence of ISAs.

The fourth market entry mode, export, basically implies that the firm operates on an arm's length basis from its home base, either through a third party (an agent, importer, distributor) or directly. The firm has no foothold in its foreign market and has no control over its distribution channels, and does not receive first hand information regarding its target market.

CONTEXTUAL AND STRATEGIC FACTORS

Industry

Industry is defined dichotomously in this study, using the Schumpeterian and Heckscher-Ohlin definitions. Firms manufacturing products containing a significant element of proprietary knowledge–knowledge which imparts unique characteristics to the product and which can be effectively withheld from competitors–act differently internationally than firms that produce products based on universal knowledge (Almor & Hirsch, 1995; Bellak, 1996; Braunerhjelm & Oxelheim, 1992; Oxelheim & Gärtner, 1996). The so called Schumpeter (S-) goods, products which are based on proprietary knowledge, are associated with installment and after sales services which depend upon firm-specific knowledge. A firm producing S-goods, which are sold in a foreign market will need to stay involved in that market in order to service its products over time. Firms producing universal or Heckscher-Ohlin (H-O) goods do not depend upon the possession of proprietary knowledge. The technology is easily acquired and does not confer a competitive advantage on the firm that possesses it. Therefore H-O firms can unbundle their value chain, as the knowledge required to service the products is in the public domain. Thus, any independent actor can service their products.

As S-goods manufacturers have to be involved in their target market, relatively to H-O goods manufacturers, it makes sense to invest in forward integration, especially when the market is situated at a geographical distance. Foreign direct investment (FDI) enables these firms to operate in a foreign market, while controlling their competitive advantages, which are embedded in the proprietary knowledge.

S-goods manufacturers will prefer wholly-owned subsidiaries over other forms because only this operation mode allows the firm to keep its knowledge proprietary. H-O manufacturers on the other hand will prefer to use other forms, which need less equity. Thus,

H1a. *S-manufacturers prefer the use of wholly-owned subsidiaries to other market entry modes in the EU market;*

H1b. *H-O-manufacturers use wholly owned subsidiaries less often than S-manufacturers as a market entry mode in the EU market.*

Ownership and Size

Firms need various resources in order to engage in international expansion. It is commonly assumed that the contextual variables such as ownership and size of the firm reflect its capability for generation of the resources needed to expand internationally (Agarwal & Ramashwami, 1992; Buckley and Casson, 1976; Kumar, 1984). Indeed, empirical evidence shows that the impact of firm size on FDI is positive (Agarwal & Ramashwami, 1992; Buckley and Casson, 1976; Yu and Ito, 1988). Thomsen and Pedersen (1996) who studied various forms of ownership modes, found that ownership structure is related among others, to the firm's size, i.e., the larger the firm, the more dispersed the ownership.

According to researchers such as Pfeffer and Salancik (1978) and Pfeffer and Nowak (1976), full hierarchical control over the incorporated resources is preferred over partial control. Thus it is expected that large firms which have relative abundant financial and other resources will invest in wholly-owned subsidiaries, while small firms have few options but to export.

As discussed before, firms that prefer to stay flexible in uncertain environment use strategic partnerships such as IJVs and ISAs; therefore it is hypothesized that the use of IJVs and ISAs are not directly related to contextual variables.

H2a. *Large firms with dispersed ownership use wholly-owned sales subsidiaries in the EU market, small firms use export as market entry strategies.*

H2b. *No relationship exists between size, ownership and the use of IJVs and ISAs.*

International Experience

Firms situated in small countries become international players at an early stage in their development, because of lack of home markets for firm-specific assets (e.g., Caves, 1982; Dunning, 1981,1988; Hymer, 1976). Research on market entry modes by firms originating in small countries has been prolific in Scandinavia. The Uppsala model proposed an incremental internationalization mode (e.g., Johanson and Wiedersheim-Paul, 1975; Johanson and Vahlne, 1977), which after twenty years still forms the basis for further research and discussion (e.g., Hedlund and Kverneland, 1985; Newbould, Buckley and Thurwell, 1978; Millington and Bayliss, 1990; Petersen and Pedersen, 1997).

The Uppsala model suggests that firms with more international experience will use FDI more frequently. International experience comes with age, i.e., the longer a company operates in the international environment the more experience it has. Firms without foreign market experience have been observed to overstate potential risks, while understating the potential returns of marketing in a foreign market. Therefore, it is more likely that firms without international experience will choose a market entry mode which is not based on FDI (Agarwal & Ramashwami, 1992; Caves and Mehra, 1986; Gatignon and Anderson, 1988). On the other hand, firms with more experience are expected to prefer modes that involve FDI.

H3. *Firms with more international experience use higher levels of FDI.*

Dependence on Foreign Markets

When firms depend mainly on foreign sales they will attempt to have more influence on the foreign market and be highly involved in that market. Pfeffer and Salancik (1978) argue that firms always seek ways to reduce dependence upon environmental factors. One way to reduce dependence is by internalizing into the organizational hierarchy (part of) those factors on which the firm depends, i.e., by integrating for instance marketing channels into the organizational hierarchy. This point is further strengthened by the transaction cost paradigm (Williamson, 1975) and the variants of internalization theory (e.g., Buckley, 1988; Rugman, 1985) as well as by empirical studies which examined firms' control patterns used in foreign markets (e.g., Anderson & Gatignon, 1986; Gatignon & Anderson, 1988; Hennart, 1991). Therefore, firms that are highly dependent upon a foreign market will use forward integration when possible in order to reduce dependence and enlarge its involvement with that market.

H4. A positive relation exists between the dependence of the firm on foreign sales and the use of FDI.

Perception of the Foreign Market

Change is one of the central aspects of the environment that is an ongoing cause of concern for decision-makers in an organization. Changing environments present the firm with uncertainty regarding the future, as well as with new opportunities and threats.

The data for this study were gathered during the beginning of the 1990s when changes were taking place in the EU as a result of Europe 1992. Creation of the Single Market caused various degrees of change in all industries in the EU. As was shown above, researchers agree that ISAs allow firms to cope with dynamic, changing and uncertain environments (Hergert and Morris, 1988; Ohmae, 1989; Porter and Fuller, 1986; Pucik, 1988). Moreover, Rivoli and Salorio (1996) showed that in uncertain environments ownership and internalization advantages are negatively rather than positively associated with FDI. Therefore,

H5. *A positive relationship exists between perception of a high degree of (a) uncertainty (b) change (c) opportunity and the use of and ISAs.*

METHOD AND DATA BASE

The data in this study are taken from the population of Israeli manufacturing firms which market their products in the European Union (EU). Although Israel has a Free Trade Agreement with the EU, Israeli firms remain outsiders (Almor and Hirsch, 1995) who have to deal with a foreign market.

Data were gathered during 1991 by means of structured interviews as well as through mailed questionnaires and were provided either by the CEO or by senior managers.

All Israeli manufacturers who reported over five million dollars in international sales in 1989 were approached and asked to participate in this study. This group included 140 firms. In addition, a sample of 50 small firms which reported revenues from international sales ranging between one and five million dollars, were also approached. Subsequently those that did not have sales in the EU or operated in defense industries were deleted. A questionnaire, which was pretested in ten firms and slightly adapted, was sent to the remaining

CEOs. Thirty-three firms returned the questionnaire, however, only 26 could be used for statistical analysis. Subsequently the non-responding exporters were approached by telephone and interviews were set up. Fifty-eight structured interviews were conducted that could be used subsequently for statistical analysis. The final sample included 84 firms, which represented approximately 70% of the whole population of Israeli manufacturers who operated in the EU market in 1990/91.

VARIABLES

Six independent variables are studied here and are listed below:

Industry

The firms in the sample were situated in twelve different industries, which were subsequently grouped into S- and H-O industries. Division of firms into S- and H-O goods manufacturers was based on data obtained from the Israel Central Bureau of Statistics.[1] According to this division 44 firms in the sample were classified as H-O and 39 as S-product manufacturers (1 missing case).

Size and Ownership

An organization's size was measured by means of four items:

- Number of employees.
- Total sales in 1990.
- Total foreign sales in 1990.
- Sales in the European Union (EU) in 1990.

Five types of ownership were studied in this paper; they included: private ownership, government, kibbutz, publicly traded, Histradrut (trade union).[2] Ownership concentration of Israeli firms is very high and nearly all firms in the sample had one dominant shareholder with a voting majority.

International Experience

International experience was tested by means of four items:

- The year the firm started selling internationally.
- The year the firm started selling in the EU.
- Time gap between establishment of the firm and international sales.
- Time gap between establishment of the firm and sales in the EU.

Dependence on Foreign Markets

Two indicators were used to measure this variable: average percentage of foreign sales and average percentage of sales in the EU during the years 1988-90. The higher the percentage the higher the dependence upon foreign markets.

Perception of the EU Environment

Three measures of environmental perception were used in this study. Each measure was created from an index comprising a number of items.

1. *Perceived uncertainty* measured the amount of uncertainty that decision-makers in the firm perceived regarding the process of unification of the European Union. The index was based on five items (alpha Cronbach ≡ .75).
2. *Environmental change* measured the degree of change perceived by the firm's decision-makers in the EU as a result of unification. The index was comprised of five items (alpha Cronbach = .77).
3. *Opportunities* concerned the degree of new opportunities in the EU as perceived by the decision-makers of the firms. The index was based on twelve items (alpha Cronbach = .77).

Market Entry Modes

The dependent variable in this study was the market entry strategy chosen by the firm to compete in the EU market. Listed below are the four strategies used in this study:

1. *Wholly-owned marketing subsidiaries* established in the EU before 1992.
2. *International joint ventures* established in the EU before 1992. International joint ventures were defined as subsidiaries that are jointly owned by an Israeli partner and at least one EU partner. Thus they were based on FDI as well as on the transfer of other resources.
3. *International strategic alliances* established before 1993. International strategic alliances only included those forms that were not based on FDI, such as cooperation agreements, projects and know-how exchange.
4. *Export* either directly or through an agent/distributor.

RESULTS

Contextual Factors and Choice of Market Entry Strategy

Cross tabulations presented in Table 1 show that fifty-nine percent of the Schumpeterian manufacturers had wholly-owned subsidiaries in the EU, and seventy four percent of this group had established more than one. Seventy percent of the H-O manufacturers exported their products to the EU and only twenty three percent established wholly owned subsidiaries. International strategic alliances were the second most frequently used operation mode by this group, thus supporting hypothesis 1.

Cross tabulations in Table 1 further show that differences exist among types of ownership and entry mode. Companies that were completely privately owned as well as those owned by kibbutzim preferred to use export. It should be said here that these firms are also characterized by their small size. Firms that were government owned and publicly traded firms and are also larger in size, preferred to use wholly owned subsidiaries. ISAs were found in high frequency among kibbutz owned firms.

T-tests presented in Table 1 show that size is related to the use of different market entry modes, thus supporting hypothesis 2. Basically, large firms used wholly-owned subsidiaries, medium sized firms used IJVs and small sized firms used export. However, the use of ISAs was not explained by size. Indeed, ISA users had the largest amount of foreign sales in 1990 compared to firms using other entry modes and

TABLE 1. Relationships Between Entry Modes, Contextual and Strategic Factors

Contextual and Strategic Factors:	Entry mode: Wholly owned subsidiary	Export	International joint venture	International strategic alliance
Industry:				
H-O	23%	70%	9%	32%
S	59% (χ2 = 10.9***)	31% (χ2 = 12.4***)	15% (χ2 = .71)	26% (χ2 = .38)
Ownership:				
Private	37% (χ2 = 0.4)	61% (χ2 = 3.1*)	2% (χ2 = 8.2**)	18% (χ2 = 5.2**)
Public	44% (χ2 = 0.2)	36% (χ2 = 3.3*)	24% (χ2 = 4.7**)	36% (χ2 = 0.9)
Government	71% (χ2 = 3.1*)	14% (χ2 = 4.2**)	14% (χ2 = 0.0)	14% (χ2 = 0.9)
Kibbutz	14% (χ2 = 2.1)	86% (χ2 = 3.6*)	14% (χ2 = 0.0)	71% (χ2 = 6.7**)
Histadrut	67% (χ2 = 0.9)	0% (χ2 = 3.3*)	100% (χ2 = 22.4**)	67% (χ2 = 2.2)
Size:				
# employees	962 (t = −4.94**)	283 (t = 4.12**)	452 (t = 1.16)	661 (t = −.87)
Total sales⊕	93 (t = −4.03**)	29 (t = 3.75**)	48 (t = .32)	75 (t = −1.80*)
Foreign sales⊕	3.0 (t = 1.8*)	3.4 (t = −1.6)	3.5 (t = −0.8)	3.6 (t = −1.7*)
EC sales⊕	2.9 (t = −1.5)	2.4 (t = 1.8*)	3.1 (t = −1.4)	3.0 (t = −2.0**)
International experience in EU:	7 years after establ. (p < .10)	12 years after establ.	5 years after establ. (p < .10)	11 years after establ. (p < .05)
Dependence on foreign markets:	73% (p < .10)	60%	74% (p < .10)	64%
Perception of EU market:				
Uncertainty	3.0 (t = 1.8*)	3.4 (t = −1.6)	3.5 (t = −0.8)	3.6 (t = −1.7*)
Change	2.9 (t = −1.5)	2.4 (t = 1.8*)	3.1 (t = −1.4)	3.0 (t = −2.0**)
Opportunity	2.0 (t = −1.1)	2.0 (t = .93)	2.2 (t = −0.8)	2.3 (t = −2.6**)

* p < .10
** p < .05
*** p < .01
⊕ in 1990 in $ M

were highly dependent upon the EU market. These findings suggest that use of ISAs is not explained by contextual variables.

Strategic Factors and Choice of Market Entry Strategy

International experience enabled to differentiate between choice of export, WOS and ISAs and IJVS. Firms that started operating in the EU market relatively early in their organizational lives (i.e., on average five years after establishment used IJVs significantly more). Firms that started somewhat later in their organizational lives (after seven years on average) used wholly-owned subsidiaries significantly more often. Firms that entered the EU market relatively late (12 years on average after establishment) used export ISAs more often. Thus, the results supported hypothesis 3 only partly.

The fourth hypothesis posed that a positive relation exists between the dependence of the firm on foreign sales and the degree of control it exercises over its foreign operations. Firms which had wholly-owned subsidiaries or IJVs in the EU were significantly dependent upon foreign sales (i.e., 73%, $p < .10$ and 74%, $p < .06$ foreign sales respectively). Firms that employed ISAs and export as international modes of operation in the EU market, were less dependent upon foreign sales (64% and 60% foreign sales respectively) thereby supporting the hypothesis.

The fifth hypothesis, which posed that a positive relationship exists between perception of a high degree of (a) uncertainty, (b) change, (c) opportunity and the use of ISAs, was supported by results presented in Table 1.

Firms that employed ISAs in the EU perceived significantly more uncertainty, change and opportunity in that environment than firms that chose other modes of operation. Firms with IJVs also perceived more uncertainty, change and opportunities than exporters and firms with wholly owned subsidiaries, however, the differences were not significant. Firms with wholly-owned subsidiaries perceived less uncertainty than other firms did and exporters discerned less change. These findings support the fifth hypothesis.

DISCUSSION

The results presented in this paper show that a contingency view of market entry strategies is indeed called for. When comparing the four entry strategies: wholly-owned marketing subsidiaries, export, international joint ventures and international strategic alliances, it is clear that each entry strategy has a different profile, as is summarized in Table 2. As hypothesized both contextual and strategic variables are related to choice of entry strategy, however, each strategy has a different configuration.

The contextual factor, which included industry, ownership and size, was related differently to each strategic option. Findings showed that

TABLE 2. Type and Level of Contextual and Strategic Factors When Employing Various Entry Modes

Entry modes:	Type of industry	Size of firm	Duration of international experience	Dependence on foreign market	Perception of foreign market
Wholly owned subsidiary	Schumpeterian	Large	Long	High	Low uncertainty, little change, little opportunity
Export	Heckscher-Ohlin	Small	Short	Low	Low uncertainty, very little change, little opportunity
International joint venture	–	Small/Medium	Long	High	Some uncertainty, much change, many opportunities
International strategic alliance	–	Medium/Large	Short	Low	High uncertainty, much change, many opportunities

industry and size were strongly related to choice of wholly-owned marketing subsidiaries and export, but not to choice of IJVs and ISAs.

When a firm's competitive advantages are based on a significant element of unique knowledge it will make an effort to keep the knowledge proprietary. The best way to do this in a foreign market is by established wholly-owned marketing subsidiaries (Almor & Hirsch, 1995; Bellak, 1996; Braunerhjelm & Oxelheim, 1992; Oxelheim & Gärtner, 1996). Indeed, findings in this study showed that firms based in Schumpeterian industries employed wholly-owned marketing subsidiaries significantly more than any other entry mode. Use of this entry mode strategy allows the firm to lower the dissemination risks, which occur when external agents or strategic partners can expropriate firm-specific advantages (Hill, Hwang and Kim, 1990).

Firms producing universal or Heckscher-Ohlin (H-O) goods, on the other hand, do not depend upon the possession of proprietary knowledge. The technology is easily acquired and does not confer a competitive advantage on the firm that possesses it. Therefore H-O firms can unbundle their value chain as the knowledge required to service the products is in the public domain, allowing the firms' products to be serviced by any independent actor. Indeed, firms situated in H-O classified industries chose export most frequently as entry mode strategy, which enabled them to operate in a foreign market without incurring the costs of establishing and managing a subsidiary or some form of a strategic alliance.

Size was a second contextual factor that was significantly related to choice of wholly-owned subsidiaries and export, but not to various types of ISAs and IJVs. Findings showed that large firms preferred to use wholly-owned marketing subsidiaries, small firms on the other hand, chose export as an entry strategy. Again, these findings are supported by literature. Root (1994) as well as John (1997) suggest that firms with limited resources, i.e., small firms, are not able to dedicate assets and the level of commitment necessary to succeed with entry mode strategies based on FDI, therefore export is the most common entry strategy used. Entry modes based on ISAs and IJVs on the other hand, were not size dependent. This finding contradicts the argument that strategic alliances are used by small firms to expand their strategic options, while using limited assets (Brooke, 1986), entering the international market by pooling tangible and intangible resources, thereby forming a *virtual* larger company (e.g., Bleeke & Ernst, 1993; Ohmae, 1989; Porter & Fuller, 1986; Powell, 1987). Results in this study clearly showed that choosing a strategic alliance as entry strategy is not based on contextual considerations such as size and industry.

International experience in and dependence upon the EU market comprised the *strategic* factor that provided explanation for choice between entry forms based on a large measure of equity and control vs. a lower measure of control. Firms that entered the EU relatively early in their organizational lives and were highly dependent upon this market established either wholly-owned marketing subsidiaries or international joint ventures. Firms that entered the EU market at a relatively late stage and were less dependent upon this market preferred export or ISAs. The findings support Johanson and Vahlne's model (1977) which argues that internationalization is a process of sequential market commitment of firm specific resources following uncertainty reduction due to the accumulation of market experience. The results also support Calof and Beamish's (1995) findings that resources and international experience explain the use of FDI. Although literature, as well as the results, explain when firms use equity based entry strategies, it does not explain when firms prefer IJVs to wholly-owned subsidiaries or ISAs over export.

A firm's entry choice between a wholly-owned subsidiary and an IJV or ISA seems to depend upon perception of the foreign market. Firms with wholly-owned subsidiaries perceive significantly less uncertainty regarding the foreign market than do those that use IJVs and ISAs. Moreover, they perceive less change and less opportunities, albeit not significantly. Firms that choose ISAs perceive significantly more uncertainty, more change and more opportunities in their business environment than do those employing any of the other entry strategies.

Theoretical support for this finding can be found among arguments such as the one raised by Pucik (1988), who maintains that firms operating in an unpredictable environment where variance of return is very large, will prefer to share the risk rather than to go it alone. Powell (1987) proposes that when the environment is very dynamic, firms will prefer alliances as a way to reposition themselves quickly without incurring the high costs associated with internalization and without loss of flexibility. Thus, findings in this study support the position that perception of the environment in terms of uncertainty or change plays an important role in the explanation of the existence of ISAs, even more so than contextual factors.

Importance of the strategic factor is further strengthened by the fact that firms in the sample did not confine themselves necessarily to one type of market entry strategy. Indeed, 13% of the firms in the sample employed both wholly owned subsidiaries as well as ISAs to enter the EU market. Israeli firms marketing their products in the EU are at a physical and psychic distance from these markets. Especially in times of change, such as unification of the EU, local partners can help reduce uncertainty regarding the change, adapt more easily to it and help recognize new opportunities created by the change. Although ISAs and IJVs reduce the amount of control a firm has over its resources and competitive advantages compared to wholly owned subsidiaries, they enable management to gain in terms of market understanding, which in the long term may lead to a more successful performance. Therefore, even firms that already have established wholly owned marketing subsidiaries employ ISAs in order to deal with a changing environment, characterized by a higher level of uncertainty and by new opportunities.

Thus, while contextual factors such as industry and size seem to be important for Israeli firms choosing entry strategies in the EU market, strategic factors such as perception of change and new opportunities seem to explain choice of strategic alliances more fully. Moreover, firms seem to choose entry modes according to configurations of both contextual and strategic factors. Findings in this study showed that a large Israeli firm with little international experience but a perception that the EU market is changing might choose some type of alliance strategy to enter the EU market. A large firm with much international experience and no perception of change in the environment may likely choose establishment of a wholly-owned marketing subsidiary to enter that same market.

Although further research is required, the findings in this study point to the direction of a contingency view of market entry strategies based on a multivariate model.

NOTES

1. The data covered employment costs per industry and the percentage of technical personnel, i.e., technicians, engineers and scientists, in the labor force of the different industrial branches. Industries with a ratio of technical to total personnel of under 15% and with monthly employment costs per employee of under $1,500 were classified as H-O goods manufacturers. Industries exceeding the ratio were classified S-goods manufacturers. Thus, chemicals, electrical and electronic industries belonged to the S-group, all other industries to the H-O group (Almor and Hirsch, 1995).

2. Private ownership, i.e., all the firm's shares are in private hands. This was the largest group in the sample, representing 52.4%.

3. Government owned, meaning that at least 50% of the firm is owned by the government. 9.5% of the sample belonged to this category.

4. Kibbutz owned means that the kibbutz owns all the firm's shares. The kibbutz is a communal form of living, which exists in Israel since the beginning of this century. People who are kibbutz members share assets, resources, ownership as well as obligations. One of the interesting features of kibbutz life is that private ownership does not exist–everything is shared according to individual needs. Although kibbutzim were traditionally engaged in agriculture, most have established factories as well. Seven firms in the sample (8.3%) were kibbutz owned companies.

5. Publicly owned firms are defined as firms that are traded on stock exchanges. The second largest group in the sample, this category included 29.8% of the firms.

6. Labor union owned firms are categorized as such if at least 50% of the firm's shares are in the hands of the Labor Union (Histadrut). Besides being Israel's largest labor union, the Histadrut also used to be Israel's largest employer and has a very large amount of assets; 3.6% of the companies in the sample were Histadrut owned.

REFERENCES

Agarwal, S. and Ramashwami, S.N. (1992). Choice of foreign market entry mode: Impact of ownership, location and internalization factors. *Journal of International Business Studies.* 23 (1): 1-27.

Almor, T. and Hirsch, S. (1995). Outsiders' response to Europe 1992: Theoretical considerations and empirical evidence. *Journal of International Business Studies.* 26 (2): 223-237.

Anderson, E. and Gatignon, H. (1986). Modes of foreign entry: A transaction cost analysis and propositions. *Journal of International Business Studies.* 17 (3): 1-26.

Bellak, C. (1996). Foreign direct investment from small states and integration: Micro- and macro-economic evidence from Austria. In: Hirsch, S. and Almor, T. (Eds.)

Outsiders' Response to European Integration. Handelshojskolens Forlag. Copenhagen, Denmark.

Bery, V. and Bowers, T.A. (1993). Rebuilding an alliance. In Bleeke, J. and Ernst, D. (eds.) *Collaborating to Compete: Using Strategic Alliances and Acquisitions in the Global Marketplace.* John Wiley & Sons, New York.

Bleeke, J. and Ernst, D. (1993). *Collaborating to Compete: Using Strategic Alliances and Acquisitions in the Global Marketplace.* John Wiley & Sons, New York.

Borys, B. and Jemison, D.B. (1989). Hybrid arrangements as strategic alliances: Theoretical issues in organizational combinations. *Academy of Management Review. 14*: 234-249.

Braunerhjelm, P. and Oxelheim, L. (1992). Heckscher-Ohlin and Schumpeter industries: The response by Swedish multinational firms to the EC 1992 program. Working paper 352. Stockholm: Industrial Institute for Economic and Social Research.

Brooke, M.Z. (1986). *International Management.* Hutchinson, London.

Buckley, P.J. (1988). The limits of explanation: Testing the internalization theory of the multinational enterprise. *Journal of International Business Studies. 19 (2):* 181-194.

Buckley, P.J. and Casson, M.C. (1986). *The Future of the Multinational Enterprise.* London: Macmillan.

Calof, J.L. (1994). The relationship between firm size and export behavior revisited. *Journal of International Business Studies. 25 (2)*: 367-387.

Calof, J.L. and Beamish, P.W. (1995). Adapting to foreign markets: Explaining internationalization. *International Business Review. 4 (2):* 115-131.

Caves, R.E. (1982). *Multinational Enterprise and Economic Analysis.* Cambridge: Cambridge University Press.

Caves, R.E. and Mehra, S.K. (1986). Entry of foreign multinationals into U.S. manufacturing industries. In Porter, M.E. (ed.) *Competition in Global Industries.* Boston: Harvard Business Press.

Chang, S.J. and Rosenzweig, P.M. (1998). Industry and regional patterns in sequential foreign market entry. *Journal of Management Studies. 35 (6):* 797-822.

Dunning, J.H. (1981). *International Production and Multinational Enterprise.* London: Allen and Unwin.

Dunning, J.H. (1988). The eclectic paradigm of international production: A restatement and some possible extensions. *Journal of International Business Studies. 19*: 1-31.

Gatignon, H.A. and Anderson, E. (1988). The multinational corporation's degree of control over foreign subsidiaries: An empirical test of a transaction cost explanation. *Journal of Law, Economics and Organization.* 4 (2): 305-336.

Hamel, G., Doz, Y.L. and Prahalad, C.K. (1988). Collaborate with your competitors–and win. *Harvard Business Review. 67*: 133-139.

Hedlund, G. and Kverneland, A. (1985). Are strategies for foreign markets changing? The case of Swedish Investment in Japan. *International Studies of Management and Organization. 15 (2):* 41-59.

Hennart, J-F. (1991). Control in multinational firms: The role of price and hierarchy. *Management International Review.* (Special Issue): 71-96.

Hergert, M. and Morris, D. (1988). Trends in international collaborative agreements. In Contractor, F.J. and Lorange, P. (Eds.) *Cooperative Strategies in International Business.* Lexington, MA: Lexington Books, pp. 99-109.

Heum, P. and Ylä-Antilla, P. (1993). *Firm Dynamics in a Nordic Perspective: Large Corporations and Industrial Transformation.* The Research Institute of the Finnish Economy. Helsinki, Finland.

Hill, C.W.L, Hwang, P. and Kim, C.W. (1990). An eclectic theory of the choice of international entry mode. *Strategic Management Journal.* 11: 117-128.

Hymer, S. (1976). *The International Operations of National Firms: A Study of Direct Foreign Investment.* Cambridge, MA. MIT Press.

Jarillo, J.C. (1988). On strategic networks. *Strategic Management Journal, 9*: 31-41.

Johanson, J. and Vahlne, J.E. (1977). The internationalization process of the firm–A model of knowledge development and increasing market commitments. *Journal of International Business Studies. 8*: 23-32.

Johanson, J. and Wiedersheim-Paul, F. (1975). The internationalization of the firm–four Swedish cases. *Journal of Management Studies, 12 (3):* 305-322.

John, R. (1997) (Ed.). *Global Business Strategy.* International Thomson Business Press, London, UK.

Karlsen, J.K. (1991). Business strategy and national policy concerning integration: Nordic direct foreign investment in the European Community. Working Paper. Business and Economic Studies on European Integration. WP 1-91.

Kim, W.C., and Hwang, P. (1992). Global strategy and multinationals' entry mode choice. *Journal of International Business Studies. 23 (1):* 29-54.

Kogut, B. and Singh, H. (1988). The effect of national culture on the choice of entry mode. *Journal of International Business Studies. 19 (3):* 411-432.

Kogut, B. and Zander, U. (1993). Knowledge of the firm and the evolutionary theory of the multinational corporation. *Journal of International Business Studies. 24 (4)*: 625-645.

Kojima, K. (1990). *Japanese Direct Investment Abroad.* Tokyo, International Christian University.

Kojima, K. and Ozawa, T. (1984). Micro- and macro-economic models of direct foreign investments: Towards a synthesis. *Hitosubashi Journal of Economics. 25*: 1-20.

Kumar, M.S. (1984). *Growth, Acquisition, and Investment: An Analysis of the Growth of Industrial Firms and their Overseas Activities.* Cambridge: Cambridge University Press.

Millington, A., and Bayliss, B. (1990). The process of internationalization: UK companies in the EC. *Management International Review. 30 (2):* 151-161.

Newbould, G., Buckley, P. and Thurwell, J. (1978). *Going International: The Experience of Smaller Companies Overseas.* Wiley and Sons, New York.

Nitsch, D., Beamish, P., and Makino, S. (1996). Entry mode and performance of Japanese FDI in Western Europe. *Management International Review. 36 (1):* 27-43.

Ohmae, K. (1989). The global logic of strategic alliances. *Harvard Business Review. 67*: 143-154.

Oxelheim, L. and Gärtner, R. (1996). Home country effects from outward FDI: A regional study of changes in production patterns. In: Hirsch, S. and Almor, T. (Eds.) *Outsiders' Response to European Integration.* Handelshojskolens Forlag. Copenhagen, Denmark.

Petersen, B. and Pedersen, T. (1997). Twenty years after–Support and critique of the Uppsala Internationalization model. In I. Björkman and M. Forsgren (Eds.) *The Nature of the International Firm.* Copenhagen Business School Press, Copenhagen, Denmark.

Pfeffer, J., & Nowak, P. (1976). Joint ventures and inter organizational dependence. *Administrative Science Quarterly. 21*: 398-418.

Pfeffer, J., Salancik, G.R. (1978). *The External Control of Organizations.* New York, Harper & Row Publ.

Porter, M.E., & Fuller, M.B. (1986). Coalitions and global strategy. In M.E. Porter (ed.) *Competition in Global Industries.* Boston, MA. Harvard Business School. pp. 315-343.

Powell, W.W. (1987). Hybrid organizational arrangements: New form or transitional development?. *California Management Review. 30*: 67-87.

Pucik, V. (1988). Strategic alliances, organizational learning, and competitive advantage: The HRM agenda. *Human Resource Management. 27*: 77-93.

Root, F.R. (1994). *Entry Strategies for International Markets.* Lexington Books, Lexington, MA.

Rivoli, P. and Salorio, E. (1996). Foreign direct investment and investment under uncertainty. *Journal of International Business Studies. 27 (2)*: 335-357.

Rugman, A.M. (1985). Internalization is still a general theory of foreign direct investment. *Weltwirtschaftliches Archiv. 121*: 570-575.

Shenkar, O. (1990). International joint ventures' problems in China: Risks and remedies. *Long Range Planning. 23*: 82-90.

Shenkar, O. and Zeira, Y. (1987). Human resource management in international joint ventures: Directions for research. *Academy of Management Review. 12*: 546-557.

Thomsen, S. and Pedersen, T. (1996). Nationality and ownership structures: The 100 largest companies in six European nations. *Management International Review. 36 (2)*: 149-166.

Williamson, O.E. (1975). *Markets and Hierarchies: Analysis and Antitrust Implications.* New York, Free Press.

Yu, C.M. and Ito, K. (1988). Oligopolistic reaction and foreign direct investment: The case of the US tire and textile industries. *Journal of International Business Studies. 19 (3)*: 449-460.

Foreign Direct Investment in Transition Economies: The Case of Coca-Cola in Russia

Robert E. Morgan
Eleri R. Thorpe

SUMMARY. The paper advances several theoretical and practical developments underlying the foreign direct investment episodes of multinational corporations in transition economies, most particularly Eastern Europe. Following this, arguments are developed and discussed concerning the liberalization of the Russian economy and the changing consumer, management, organizational, and investment traditions therein. A case example of the Coca-Cola Company in Russia is both presented and analyzed. Reference is made to the experience of this company con-

---

Robert E. Morgan is Chair in Marketing and Strategic Management, School of Management and Business, University of Wales Aberystwyth, Cledwyn Building, Penglais, Aberystwyth SY33 3DD United Kingdom (E-mail: robert.morgan@ aber.ac. uk). Eleri R. Thorpe is affiliated with the School of Management and Business, University of Wales, Aberystwyth Cledwyn Building Penglais Aberystwyth SY33 3DD United Kingdom

The authors gratefully acknowledge the management and staff of Coca-Cola Refreshments (Moscow) for their help and assistance in completing this study. The cooperation of Mr. Iwan Williams, and many other senior executives is particularly appreciated, as is the support of Ms. Olga Petrova.

The views and opinions expressed in this paper are the authors' own (except where acknowledged citations are given) and do not necessarily represent those of the Coca-Cola Company.

[Haworth co-indexing entry note]: "Foreign Direct Investment in Transition Economies: The Case of Coca-Cola in Russia." Morgan, Robert E., and Eleri R. Thorpe. Co-published simultaneously in *Journal of Euromarketing* (International Business Press, an imprint of The Haworth Press, Inc.) Vol. 10, No. 1, 2001, pp. 27-48; and: *Foreign Direct Investment and Strategic Alliances in Europe* (ed: Hong Liu) International Business Press, an imprint of The Haworth Press, Inc., 2001, pp. 27-48. Single or multiple copies of this article are available for a fee from The Haworth Document Delivery Service [1-800-342-9678, 9:00 a.m. - 5:00 p.m. (EST). E-mail address: getinfo@haworthpressinc.com].

cerning its: market entry; market development; market expansion; strategic problems and barriers to expansion; and, late versus first-mover advantages in an emerging market of this transition economy. Various conclusions are drawn from this case and inferences are made for theoretical developments and company strategy in the specific field of foreign direct investment in transition economies.

KEYWORDS. Foreign direct investment, market entry strategy, strategic options, market development, market expansion, transition economies, Russia, Coca-Cola

INTRODUCTION

The proliferation of global markets is calling for a new marketing imperative which presents new challenges and threats to international companies. No sanctuary can be found from these forces and companies are faced with no alternative but to face up to the reality that not only is the form of customer-markets changing rapidly but that regulatory, political, and, socio-cultural changes are taking place at levels without precedent. The accelerated growth, and subsequent decline, of the East-Asia "tiger" economies, the stabilization of previously volatile economies of the industrializing world, the perpetual growth witnessed by highly evolved economies, the increasingly important role played by trading area agreements and blocs such as NAFTA, EU, and the ASEAN, are all overshadowed by the opening up of (former) Communist economies to international trade and more open-competition. Collectively referred to as transition economies, documentary evidence is emerging in the international business literature as to the origins, development, inertia, and implications of the movement towards freer markets in these contexts, particularly those of economies of the Soviet successor states, China, Vietnam, Poland, Hungary, Bulgaria, and the Czech and Slovak Republics to name a few (Glowacki, 1991; Reddy, 1991; Hare, 1993; Marinov, Cox, Avlonitis, and Kouremenos, 1993; Wright, Filatotchev, and Buck, 1993; Buckley and Ghauri, 1994).

This paper aims to review several theoretical and practical developments underlying the foreign direct investment episodes of multinational corporations in such transition economies. Moreover, arguments are developed and discussed concerning the liberalization of the Russian economy and the changing consumer, management, organizational, and investment traditions therein. A case example of the Coca-Cola Company in Russia is discussed which presents an account of the "experience" of this organization in terms of its market entry; market development; market expansion; strategic problems and barriers to expansion; and, late- versus first-mover advantages in an emerging market of this transition economy. From this case analysis, various conclusions are drawn and inferences are made for theoretical developments and company strategy in the specific field of foreign direct investment in transition economies.

TRANSITION ECONOMIES

Any attempt to characterize transition economies is fraught with difficulty. Not only do such economies vary significantly from one to another, but each is subject to constant overwhelming change. Therefore, a definitive framework of the transition economy has to be subject to both these caveats and necessary generalizations. From the selected literature on this topic, it can be suggested that transition economies share certain base-line characteristics.

First, diminished private income is common. For instance, recent reports indicated per capita income, per annum, in China is $500 while this rises to between $2K-$4K in Central and Eastern European nations (Batra, 1997). Second, a small amount of private savings tends to be the norm. Within the context of hyperinflation experienced at various points in the development of many transition economies, negative interest rates have been set acting as a disincentive to save. Furthermore, macroeconomic factors influence banking activity to such an extent that accumulated savings in economies can be wiped out. For instance, the value of bank deposits in the former Soviet system of 1990 was equivalent to 34% of nominal GDP; two years later this proportion fell to 3% (Slater, 1996). Other macroeconomic conditions that are found include foreign trade deficits, considerable unemployment, high costs of capital, low labor costs, significant levels of indirect taxation, high import duties, harsh foreign exchange restrictions and inconvertibility (Kornai, 1980; Mascarenhas, 1982). Third, political, regulatory, administrative, and legal problems are often evident. A lack of development in systems and procedures may give way to bureaucratic obstacles, corruption and so on in the face of inappropriate mechanisms for decision making and control (Zurawicki and Becker, 1994). Fourth, seller power predominates commercial transactions and exchanges (Samiee, 1993). With demand levels outstripping supply, price-control policies are employed to constrain the open market and a preoccupation with a goods shortage philosophy tends to become apparent among consumers (Frazier, Gill, and Kale, 1989; Shama, 1992). Consequently, alternative supply approaches are adopted and gray markets emerge with imported products competing directly with comparator products from "legitimate" channels of distribution (Mueller, Wenthe, and Baron, 1993). Finally, distribution channels are diverse, fragmented and laden with multiple intermediaries. Given the geographic considerations of certain countries such as Russia and China, it is natural that distribution problems will arise often associated with a lack of commercial development as well as transportation and logistics infrastructure constraints (Reinganum and Helsell, 1994; Business Central Europe, 1995).

While these are typical characteristics of transition economies, a clear distinction emerges when compared with command and market economies. Figure 1 illustrates the salient attributes exhibited by such modes of economic development according to the political, economic, and socio/cultural levels of analysis.

Following Shama (1994), it can be seen that the pattern of change from command economies to free market-based economic conditions is a process that requires transformation in every respect. Such a metamorphosis demands that the political, economic, and sociocultural changes are synchronized so as to ensure gradual and systematic evolutionary change (Slater, 1996). Case examples abound where the momentum for change has been considerable at one level (e.g., political level), while resistance has been encountered at another level (e.g., socio/cultural level) or the foundations for economic progress have not been formed appropriately (e.g., economic level). The speed of economic transition through these modes (Figure 1) tends to be slow and subject to many influences. For certain countries, this transition has been witnessed as a positive and encouraging stage in the history of such nations while, for others, considerable problems have been encountered and challenges have emerged to severely test the motivation of economies, to become "democratic," free markets founded upon "capitalist" ideologies (cf. Shama, 1994). An example of the latter is Russia, which has enjoyed considerable prosperity, albeit from a con-

FIGURE 1. Planned, Transition, and Market Economy Profiles: A Transition Perspective

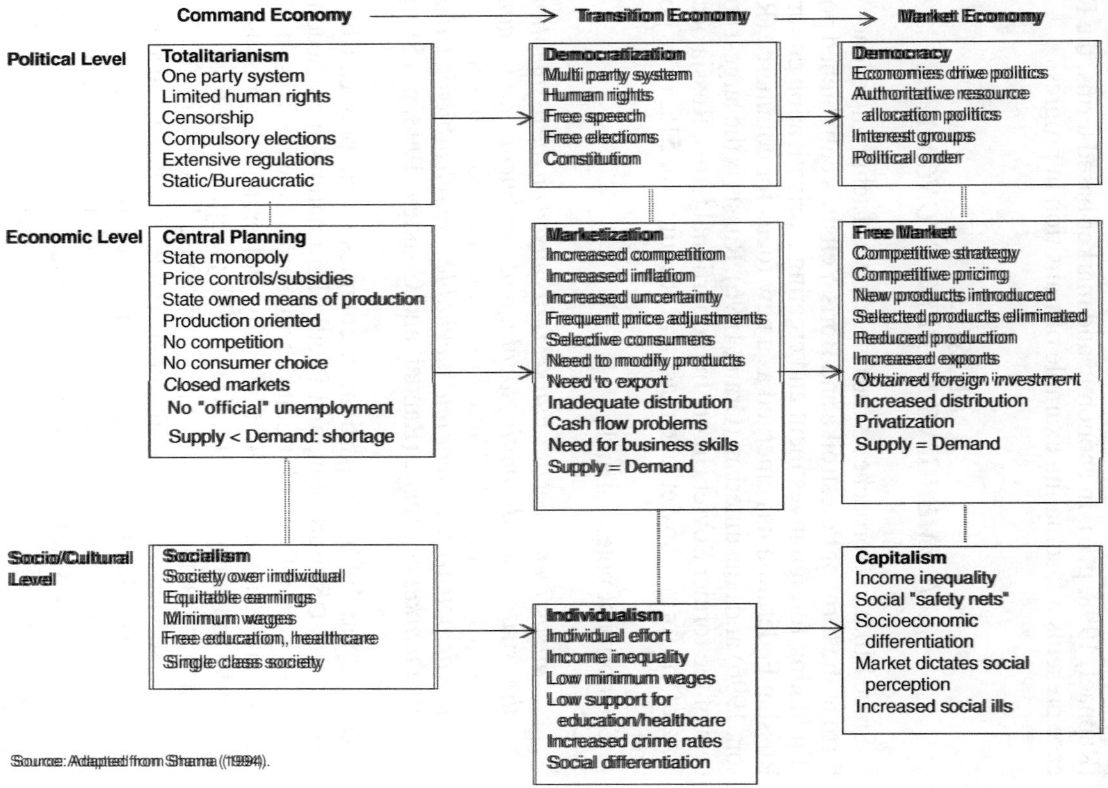

Source: Adapted from Shama (1994).

strained initial position of development, only to be handicapped by repeated problems that are reflected in its "bleak economic landscape" (Raphael, 1998, p. 6). In economic and market-based terms, the Russia case presents a fascinating example of transition in progress.

RUSSIA: AN EMERGING MARKET ECONOMY?

Since Mikhail Gorbachev's measures toward achieving economic reform in the form of Perestroika and Boris Yeltsin's enlightened policies stimulating foreign investment and creating a privatization culture, the Russian Federation has emerged as a new focus for commerce (Robinson, 1996) and consumerism (Oram, 1996). Russia is the largest constituent of the former Soviet Union. In proportional terms, Russia occupies 76% of the former Soviet land mass and accounts for 51% of its population.

The dormant potential and:

> *. . . attractiveness of this market is premised on the assumption that the swift and dramatic ideological, political, and economic changes of Yeltsin's "New Russia" and the former Soviet republics demonstrate a clear and inevitable, though difficult, transition to a market economy.* (Randall and Coakley, 1998, p. 15)

During the 1990s, in particular, countless examples can be cited where many US, European, and Pacific-Rim nations have become involved in some form of trading arrangements with Russia (Nigh, Walters, and Kuhlman, 1990; McCarthy, Puffer, and Simmonds, 1993; Tourevski and Morgan, 1993; Kvint, 1994; Adjubei, 1996).

Russian consumers have enjoyed increased exposure to Western products, services, branding, media, lifestyle and allied concept which have emerged (Batra, 1997). A consequence of this is that consumer expectations have risen in direct response to global mass media, tourism, the export and mystique of "foreign" popular culture and the marketing activities of multinational corporations (Ger and Belk, 1996). Beyond this, demand has been placed upon the management of Russian enterprises to face the commercial realities and become equipped for the "new environment of competition, efficiency, and innovation" (Czinkota, 1997, p. 73). According to Shama and Merrell (1997), responses have already become evident:

> Emerging Russian management is market oriented, so that forces of consumer demand and market supply influence management practices in order to optimize profit. Managers in this market driven pattern tend to develop new traits and managerial styles, changing from directors to managers. Increasingly, Russia's emerging managers have professional education, favor change, are active, flexible and open-minded, and market and consumer oriented. They have sales backgrounds, are strategic and entrepreneurial risk-takers, and are paid for performance. (p. 322)

This change has been slow to dawn but such developments must be tempered with the traditional context of commercial enterprise that considers references to "businessman" and "enterprise" to be synonymous with "outlaw" and "thief" (Snavely, Miassoedov, and McNeilly, 1998). Even though conventional Western business principles and practices have been slow to take hold and a recent study of the educational profile of Russian managers found that the fundamental areas of behavioral change necessary for further reforms need to be problem solving, decision making, customer orientation, team building, communication and presentation (Czinkota, 1997). All these are fundamental to successful organization management and Czinkota (1997) further identified the elements of business education considered most necessary by Russian managers: marketing, strategic planning, international business, financial analysis, and business law. Interestingly, this study also found that these areas of management development are paralleled by the factors that managers most frequently agree will provide challenges for the new economic order in Russia. Shama (1994) cites the following as transformative adjustments that managers will be required to address in order to secure greater competitiveness, for example: attention to market orientation; more customer responsiveness; improved product quality; increased productivity; competitive pricing; greater use of promotion; better distribution; more merchandising; export development to the West; and, the *most important* element, the search for foreign investors.

There are several considerations that can be drawn from much of the research presenting Russia as an evolving market economy. By and large, the potential market is vast as are commercial opportunities. Some 15,000 international joint ventures are operating in Russia in addition to approximately 100,000 resident Western managers. Income levels are generally rising, rapidly changing consumer expectations are apparent, business conditions are improving, and education level of the population is high (Batra, 1997; Czinkota, 1997; Snavely et al., 1998).

Although instability of many kinds is a threat for foreign investment, the transformation programs planned are inevitably going to lead to difficulties before the benefits are experienced. Attracting FDI has been vitally important to the growth prospects of this country and the following section explores its role and the various market entry vehicles available for Russia.

FOREIGN DIRECT INVESTMENT IN RUSSIA

The vast volume of literature documenting extant issues concerned with FDI has been characterized as inconsistent and diverse with explanatory views on FDI ranging from theories of international investment (MacDougall, 1960) through to diversification theory (Lessard, 1974). In development terms, the literature on FDI originated in the 1960s with the theories of both industrial organization and monopolistic advantages (Hymer, 1960; Kindleberger, 1969) and the product life cycle (Vernon, 1966). The principal focus of this work centered around the market entry strategies of exporting versus FDI (Buckley and Casson, 1998). The 1970s witnessed the internationalization debate (Buckley and Casson, 1976) identifying licensing, franchising and subcontracting as alternative market entry vehicles. The so-called mega-merger mayhem and acquisition episodes of the 1980s revealed the distinction between international expansion via organic development or by inter-firm combinations. This decade also experienced the significant growth of international joint venture arrangements where firms were able to collaborate to compete (Fey and Beamish, 2000). Despite the growing incidence of international joint ventures through the world, the 1990s has become recognized for the role of FDI in transition economies. According to Buckley and Casson (1998) this theme,

> . . . has brought back into focus some of the classic issues of the 1960s: the "costs of doing business abroad" and the importance of "psychic distance." It has renewed interest in the general question as to why some modes of entry offer lower costs than others, and why certain circumstances seem to favor certain modes over others. (p. 540)

Although an extensive review of the development of FDI theory is beyond the scope of this article, interested readers are encouraged to read Buckley and Casson (1998) for such a review and a proposed framework for analysis.

While Russia's cumulative flow of FDI between 1988-95 amounted to $16bn, this sum is relatively small when compared with other countries that have been significantly more competitive. For example, Hungary has attracted an FDI stock of $13bn over the same period–this with a country significantly smaller than Russia and with only 7% of its population. Czinkota (1997) observes that the,

> *sparse flow of FDI capital into Russia is the result of low profitability levels of early foreign entrants into Russia, due to problems with the quality of the workforce of management, and of information. A workforce and management who understand the operations of a market economy make investment attractive. Information that provides business plans and comparable data for investors is crucial for investment efficiency. (p. 75)*

Such problems have recently been couched within the context of internal economic pressures within the country, the crash of August, 1998, and the subsequent suspension of the International Monetary Fund lending program to Russia (Thornhill, 1999). Russia's transition to a market economy is not expected to be smooth but a number of leading multinational enterprises have "shown the way" by their investment in the country. The US-Russian Business Council has hundreds of corporate members and, with the inclusion of other such similar bodies, some of the world's leading players have considered Russia to be an intrinsic part of their global market coverage. The entry strategies that these firms have engaged to break into the Russian market are varied. This type of strategic decision is fundamental to the expansion plans and possibilities for growth within the target market. Indeed Kumar and Subramaniam (1997) have gone so far as to suggest that the mode of entry decision is "*. . . one of the most critical strategic decisions for the firm. It effects all future decisions and operations of the firm in that country market*" (p. 54). McCarthy and Puffer (1997) propose a typology of FDI strategy with specific reference to Russia. Figure 2 provides an illustration of these investment modes.

Each of these strategic types reflect both the decreasing degree of strategic flexibility while simultaneously accounting for greater levels of commitment to the target market. The historical export strategy approach follows the legacy of the former commitment era where relationships were laid down in the past and customer demand was serviced

FIGURE 2. Strategic Approaches to FDI in Russia

STRATEGIC FDI TYPOLOGY	INVESTMENT CHARACTERISTICS	EXAMPLES
Limited investment strategies		
Historical export strategy	High flexibility; risk avoidance; strong market presence; building value chain elements but no production; corporate strategy of production centralized elsewhere; slow to invest directly.	Caterpillar; General Electric
Toehold strategy	High flexibility; risk avoidance; limited initial competition; less developed markets.	General Motors; Pratt & Whitney
Medium incremental strategies		
Reverse incremental investment strategy	Flexibility for redeployment of resources; availability of Russian distributors or other value chain partners; reaction to changes in legal and political environment.	IBM
Medium incremental investment strategy	Flexibility orientation; managing risk in the Russian environment; recognize increasing market receptivity; localized markets; often service-based companies.	AT&T; Chase Manhattan Bank; "Big Six" Accounting Firms
Heavy initial investment strategies		
Voluntary heavy initial investment strategy	Optimistic view of industrial or consumer market; market share objective of first or early mover; reduced flexibility; high risk; extensive global competition.	Coca-Cola; PepsiCo; McDonald's; Gillette
Forced heavy initial investment strategy	No choice for global players; no flexibility; high risk; few big global competitors.	Mobil Oil; Occidental Petroleum; Chevron; Exxon; Texaco

Source: Adapted from McCarthy and Puffer (1997).

by production requiring importation. For many firms this approach was successful and it has generated attractive returns. The toehold strategy is suited to those firms which are reluctant to invest in Russia but recognize that they need to fund the minimum required to service market need. This form of go-slow approach is one that attracts limited risk but also generates only a conservative gain.

Incremental investment strategy exemplifies the mode of investment behavior where a gradual build up of investment is appropriate but this investment can be curtailed or reversed (reverse incremental investment strategy) without losing a significant volume of the prior funds invested. The final set of strategies require heavy initial investment of either a voluntary or forced nature. The former approach is similar to that of incremental investment, with the characteristic difference being that the firm here considers the evolution of markets, competition, industry environment and so on, to warrant heavy initial investment in order to capitalize on commercial opportunities. The latter, forced heavy initial investment approach demands significant funds before there is any opportunity of commercial success. Restricted to particular industrial sectors, such as extractive natural resources, there are significant risks attracted to this approach and this mode of investment behavior is only open to certain types of proven global businesses.

Of all these investment strategies, the voluntary heavy initial investment option is particularly interesting within the context of Russia. Given the size of the potential market and general limited competition, such a venture would appear seductive to new entrants. However, juxtaposed to this view, Russia remains very much in transition as an economy suggesting that heavy investments may be appropriate for only long term return. The remainder of this article examines one particular case in point: the Coca-Cola Company in Russia and their voluntary heavy initial investment approach.

THE COCA-COLA COMPANY IN RUSSIA

Market Entry

Pepsi's successful entry into Russia began in 1960 and fueled the Coca-Cola Company's desire for access to the vast Russian market. Pepsi opened its first plant in 1974 after signing a trade agreement, with President Nixon's assistance two years earlier, based upon a counter-trade agreement in which it produced soft drinks and exported Stolichnaya® vodka. Coca-Cola also attempted entry in much the same way, but were ultimately unsuccessful. Coca-Cola seemed to be viewed as an icon of American imperialism, making it harder still to gain successful entry in the polarized political atmosphere then in existence. However, during the mid-1980s, Michael O'Neill, a diplomat and

Coca-Cola representative in Russia, began establishing influential contacts within and outside the Soviet Government. He finally managed to organize counter-trade agreements with various businesses throughout the country, the process aided considerably through governmental contacts. Perhaps the most common mistake U.S. firms have made in the early years in Russia was to enter into joint ventures to manufacture their product locally. These agreements often became mired in litigation, tax problems, and even extortion. The "best" step, according to Coca-Cola, is almost always the agent/distributor relationship and to establish a multitude of informal partners. This is not to suggest that joint ventures do not play a role in the post market entry behavior of Coca-Cola (in fact their evolutionary pattern indicates quite the contrary), but that their experience in the case of Russia was initially laden with tactical and operational difficulties in this respect.

Top management dispatched Coca-Cola representatives to Russia with the charge that in six months they needed a production and distribution system in place. Their undertaking was to convince local bottlers in strategic positions throughout the whole of Russia to begin producing Coca-Cola in their beer plants. Most independent bottlers were also bottling for Pepsi by this time as well as their own local beer. The Coca-Cola Company provided incentives for the bottlers to also begin bottling Coca-Cola through means of increased revenue. Of the enormous proliferation of companies that compete in the international business arena, very few do so by adopting the multi-local approach. At the heart of this is "the bottler system" of the Coca-Cola Company. This unique concept is often pointed to as the single factor most responsible for the global popularity of Coca-Cola. Bottling plants are, with certain exceptions, locally owned and operated by independent business people who are authorized to sell products of the Coca-Cola Company. Their charter is to bottle and sell the Company's soft drinks within certain territorial boundaries and under conditions that ensure the highest standards of product quality and uniformity.

Coca-Cola's initial phase of entry into Russia was piecemeal. Their main priority was to establish a production and distribution basis for future long-term growth. The strategy was initially to build a strong foundation and an infrastructure upon which the Company could build. Coca-Cola solely sought to expand horizontally, believing that the establishment of product presence was more important primarily than advertising and promotion. This is a remarkable departure from the strategies of companies such as Mars or Marlboro who tend to concentrate on the promotion of their brands without spending any resources on the production of their product within the host country itself. To a large extent this is a function of the product-type.

Coca-Cola, along with many other multinational corporations entering Russia during this period, required the establishment of a headquarters in the main cities of Moscow and St. Petersburg. From this, Coca-Cola's strategy was to create a presence in key cities throughout the whole of Russia's regions. Coca-Cola executives managed to persuade local bottlers in key locations to produce Coca-Cola where the company could lease, on a contractual basis, the equipment needed by the bottler to produce the soft drink, carefully guided and with stringent standards set for these overseas partners. To maintain control, Coca-Cola generally invests in these partners and spent more than U.S.$2.0 billion in joint ventures worldwide in the 1980s. In 1991, the Coca-Cola Company officially entered the Russian market and their offices moved from their previous location in Germany to the Russian capital, Moscow.

Market Development

1994 saw the second phase of development for Coca-Cola when, due to rapid growth, the resources of local bottlers became constrained. Coca-Cola gained the opportunity to begin establishing its own infrastructure away from the bottlers. It began providing more and more incentives for the local bottlers to work exclusively for Coca-Cola. Unusually, they decided to establish joint ventures with some of the existing bottlers, bought others so that they became wholly owned by Coca-Cola, and began building their own production plants. By this time, Coca-Cola's own established bottlers elsewhere in the world, such as Dunlogan (based in the U.K.), EFES (based in Turkey), and Inchcape (an international conglomerate based in the U.K.), were prepared to enter Russia. These multinational partners helped bring Coca-Cola beyond Moscow and St. Petersburg, where only a few multinationals had ventured up until that time. The Coca-Cola Company tends to rely heavily on its main bottlers when investing in large countries, such as China, due to the level of dependability and investment they can provide. In a country the size of Russia, this type of arrangement is perhaps the best way to succeed. The focus of entry began to shift towards building, constructing, and purchasing equipment along with developing production. Coca-Cola's volume increased rapidly, driven largely by its expanding production infrastructure and lateral growth through the opening of more depots, and through geographic distribution.

Market Expansion

Currently, internal developments are still being put into place so as to bring Russian operations up to speed with its global counterparts and so that Coca-Cola Russia becomes as competitive and efficient as its parent company across the world. Coca-Cola has now progressed from its phase of establishment to the stage of focusing on the consumer and marketing. This signifies a period of vertical expansion; Coca-Cola management feel that their product is becoming within "easy reach" of the Russian consumer it is now time to actively "sell" the product to the consumer. Yearly average consumption per capita in Russia is twenty units of Coke, while the worldwide average stands at two hundred, indicating *ceteris paribus* the scope that remains within the market itself.

It was felt that the marketing concept should be set up at a slow pace so as to gradually familiarize the Russian consumer; television advertising has only been employed recently with the communications strategy being a "softly-softly" approach. Can and bottle promotions were utilized initially as well as the distribution of vast quantities of point-of-sale material. It was felt that an incremental style would yield greater benefits without restricting the limited budget. Marketing success was attributed to the fact that Russian consumers had not been exposed to any significant means of marketing communication in the past. Coca-Cola has now doubled its sales volume in Russia every year for the past four years.

In less than six years, the Russian consumer has had to understand the Coca-Cola ideal and become familiar with the world's most successful brand founded upon one hundred years of advertising. Although Coca-Cola's marketing strategy is maintained on a global scale, tailoring is only made in terms of language translation on a local basis. For Coca-Cola to gain the affection and respect of Russian consumers there was a need to obtain a thorough insight into Russian values and show infinite respect towards Russian culture. To do otherwise would have been to reinforce the perception of invasive American imperialism and risk failure. As such, Coca-Cola turned its attention recently to Russian folklore in its "Drink the Legend" television campaigns and has become increasingly involved in local, community events in Russia. It has youth programmes and actively aids Russian cultural heritage by funding museums and restoration initiatives.

Strategic Problems and Barriers to Expansion

Unlike more timid multinational companies, Coca-Cola moved deliberately to overcome barriers to its expansion. As for its overall global success, Coca-Cola is known to have one of the world's most sophisticated marketing strategies. Coca-Cola beverages are the classic examples of differentiated product competition, and each market calls for mass, but often localized, marketing and promotion.

In 1996 staff were employed to implement an information system network for the Russian operation. This would effectively link the bottling plants all over the country via satellite so that the organization as a whole could operate more effectively. In terms of information technology, it can be said that Moscow and St. Petersburg are today on a par with any other city in the world. Unfortunately, in other, more rural, areas of Russia bottling plants still have to be contacted by mail or through unreliable, complicated telephone operator connections.

The lack of a stable legal system in Russia means that the Russian Coca-Cola operation has its own in-house legal team. Russian law can take many forms; statute, parliamentary decrees, and contractual documents. To add to this complexity, most of the laws are in conflict and a system of precedent hardly exists at all. Coca-Cola was forced to implement its own land leasing and registering system, which is now being implemented by the government. Coca-Cola also prides itself on paying its taxes and other corporate dues. Their commitment to avoid Mafia bribes proves to the local community that Coca-Cola respects, and is actively involved in, the restoration of the Russian economy and is committed to provide employment.

The first main thrust of Coca-Cola's entry strategy into Russia was to concentrate on production and distribution before embarking upon any form of vertical progression. The second was to ensure that there was an exceptional managerial team. Managerial quality was vital, but in a country such as Russia this was somewhat of a problem. Although native Russians are highly educated and talented, they were obviously lacking in the experience and knowledge of market forces and struggled with concepts such as marketing and promotion. In this respect, it was crucial to import Western management in key positions so as to ensure successful entry and post-entry developments. The difficulty lay in attracting and securing the best personnel for the job. These talented, prospective employees are rare and are potentially even less willing to relocate to a country such as Russia to work. The strategy, at the point when vertical expansion was embarked upon, was to only employ those staff under the age of thirty or recent graduates. Coca-Cola felt that the mind-set of younger people was not yet pre-conditioned and thus would be more receptive to accept fresh ways of thinking and of doing things. It is anticipated that in the future, Russians themselves will have gained the necessary experience and skills to secure the higher posts within the organization.

With regard to the Russian consumer, there are generally perceived to be two distinct types: those who yearn for Western products and services due to their typical superior quality, design, and reputation; and, those who tend to remain loyal and patriotic to their country. Russians as a whole are very proud of their country, are very nationalistic, and do not take kindly to the Western attitude of regarding Russian ways and practices as redundant. There are many that feel that Russia has been "destroyed" due to the assisted collapse of Communism by the West, and that their country has been unnecessarily fragmented. This attitude is not only held by the elderly but is also the belief of the young also. However, most forward-thinking Russians can appreciate the benefits and the improvements Western companies make and bring to the country. They can, and do, appreciate that foreign investment is the only way forward for Russia. On the other hand, traditionalist Russians are skeptical and remain fearful of change; they have a Soviet past and are less broad-minded, making it difficult for them to progress into a market oriented future.

Pepsi was obviously a pre-entry threat for Coca-Cola due to its longstanding presence in Russia. Coca-Cola benefitted from the fact that the Pepsi product being produced was of a low quality, and the machinery and equipment being used was dated and unreliable. Although initially Coca-Cola was bottled in Soviet standard glass beer bottles, they were prompt in updating and improving the bottling plants that they utilized which meant that the consumer did not associate Coca-Cola with such problems. Pepsi suffered as locals did not perceive it as a U.S. product. When Coca-Cola emerged with the benefit of its brand name and image it had an untarnished reputation in spite of it being produced locally. In 1996, Coca-Cola overtook Pepsi's leadership position in Russia. Today, Pepsi, although in the past preferring to utilize local bottlers, have begun production themselves and are currently in the process of constructing a plant in Moscow. Pepsi provides competition for Coca-Cola on a worldwide basis and as such cannot be disregarded due to their previous inflexibility. Although Pepsi are still second in countries such as Poland, Romania, and Albania, where they were once leaders, they are always a potential threat to Coca-Cola and the reason why defensive strategies are now being put in place.

Coca-Cola has a presence all over the world and, as such, it was not an option of whether or not to invest in Russia. The potential market was so attractive and vast that it was not an option to overlook its potential advantages. Coca-Cola invested heavily into Russia primarily because it had the resources to enable it to do so (see "Heavy initial investment strategies in Figure 2"). To avoid the risk of embarrassing failure, a company with a global reputation such as Coca-Cola cannot afford to enter a country in an incremental fashion. A large investment, therefore, had to be made due to the sheer size of the country and in order to improve the potential for success. Coca-Cola could not ignore the Russian market because their main worldwide opponents were already in position, and to leave entry until the economic situation had stabilized could have been too late. While seeking to secure late-mover advantages, foreign direct investment in Russia provided a new source of long-term growth for Coca-Cola shareholders and so a large sum was made available for the initial investment.

Late- versus First-Mover Advantages

Why has Coca-Cola found success where others have not? The answer lies in a set of short-term advantages and long-term strategic thinking. In the short term, Coca-Cola received a tax holiday from the Federal Government. This provided key space for establishment while the long-term plans for expansion were put into place. These plans included steps to: localize production, developing flexible supplier networks; and, balancing domestic and international interests helping to reduce the risk of shifting taxes and import duties.

Coca-Cola clearly demonstrates the benefits of foreign direct investment in Russia. It was instrumental in establishing market oriented, customer driven production linkages. Previously, the country knew only a Communist Party-led command system where managers were concerned about quotas alone, not customers or marketing. Production efficiency, regular delivery, and consistent quality were unfamiliar concepts let alone conceivable realities. On this score, Coca-Cola was critical in Russia's transition to capitalism.

The future for Coca-Cola in Russia is firstly a period of consolidation. A reduction in the number of bottlers would reduce costs considerably. It is likely that in the future, Coca-Cola will only utilize two or three main bottling companies, much the same as with Coca-Cola bottlers who already bottle for most of Europe. The consolidation phase should also incorporate marketing plans to encourage repeat buying and those already purchasing to buy more. Now that Coca-Cola's infrastructure is established, distribution and availability has grown and is still growing, points of availability are now crucial for Coca-Cola's continuing success.

Trade in Russia is continuing to develop, bringing new potential channels of distribution for Coca-Cola. The Cola wars will inevitably heat up in Russia as they have in every other country. Pepsi and other local brands are getting stronger, meaning that there is a need for experienced people within Coca-Cola to accommodate these new competitors and design strategic responses. Although the beverage industry is under developed in Russia, there is a consensus that a huge potential exists. Consumption is likely to increase dramatically, the speed of this being dictated by price. As the overall outlook is optimistic, it is crucial for Coca-Cola to maintain its leadership position by developing its infrastructure and consumption levels and by investing in Russian talent.

CONCLUSIONS

This paper has attempted to advance several theoretical and practical developments underlying the foreign direct investment episodes of multinational corporations in transition economies with particular reference to the Coca-Cola Company in Russia. The principal themes discussed were the "market entry," "market development," "market expansion," "strategic problems and barriers to expansion," and "late-versus. first-mover advantage" aspects of this company's since entering Russia in the 1980s. Although unique to the Coca-Cola Company, the issues presented are remarkably similar to those encountered by other companies pursuing aggressive growth strategies in emerging markets: supply chain and distribution concerns; risk in consumer perception; brand awareness and "educating" consuming publics; manufacture and production problems in terms of efficiency, quality, and reliability; new forms of competitive behavior; global strategy with local idiosyncrasies; and, professional management and worker placement considerations.

Beyond the enormous economic and political ramifications of transition, the development of Coca-Cola in Russia has not been smooth and there have been inevitable strategic considerations that have warranted close attention such as consumer and market influences. Nonetheless, the future prosperity of the Russian economy must determine the potential success of corporate penetration by Western companies. Although oscillations in salient economic indicators are inevitable, prevailing evidence suggests that Russia is likely to experience take-off at some point in the future. The question for companies to concern themselves with, therefore, is how best to position themselves for future expansion when economic transformation arrives. While there are many examples of difficulties in transition, Eastern Europe has many examples of industry-level success in certain countries and even overwhelming national success-stories in the form of Poland and Hungary, among others. Indications suggest that companies from many consumer, industrial, manufacturing and service-based, and high-/low-tech industries recognize the potential benefits from entering Russia at the present time and are thus convinced in the opinion that it is better to have at least a toehold in an emerging market than no involvement at all.

REFERENCES

Aaker, D.A., & Day, G.S. (1986). The perils of high growth markets. *Strategic Management Journal*, 7, 409-421.

Abjubei, Y. (1996). Russia: A largely untapped potential. In P. Artisien-Maksimenko & Y. Abjubei (eds.), *Foreign investment in Russia & other Soviet successor states*, (pp. 111-156). New York, NY: St. Martin's Press.

Agarwal, S., & Ramaswami, S.N. (1992). Choice of foreign market entry mode: impact of ownership, location, and internationalization factors. *Journal of International Business Studies*, 23 (1), 1-27.

Baker, M.J., & Becker, S.H. (1997). Pioneering new geographic markets. *Journal of Marketing Management*, 13 (1), 89-104.

Batra, R. (1997). Marketing issues and challenges in transitional economies. *Journal of International Marketing*, 5 (4), 95-114.

Blonigen, B.A., & Ohno, Y. (1998). Endogenous protection, foreign direct investment, and protection-building trade. *Journal of International Economics*, 46 (2), 205-227.

Borensztein, E., Gregorio, J. De., & Lee, J.W. (1998). How does foreign direct investment affect economic growth? *Journal of International Economics*, 46 (1), 115-135.

Buckley, P.J., & Casson, M.C. (1976). *The future of the multinational enterprise*. London: Holmes & Meier.

Buckley, P.J., & Casson, M.C. (1998). Analyzing foreign market entry strategies: extending the internationalization approach. *Journal of International Business Studies*, 29 (3), 539-562.

Buckley, P.J., & Ghauri, P. (1994). *The economics of change in East and Central Europe*. London: Academic Press.

Business Central Europe (1995). Transitory problems. (May). *Transport & distribution survey: Business Central Europe*, 37-50.

Chen, H., & Chen, T.J. (1998). Network linkages and location choice in foreign direct investment. *Journal of International Business Studies*, 29 (3), 445-468.

Cui, G. (1998). The evolutionary process of global market expansion: experiences of MNCs in China. *Journal of World Business*, 33 (1), 87-110.

Czinkota, M.R. (1997). Russia's transition to a market economy: learning about business. *Journal of International Marketing*, 5 (4), 73-93.

Driscoll, A.M., & Paliwoda, S.J. (1997). Dimensionalizing international market entry mode choice. *Journal of Marketing Management*, 13 (1), 57-87.

Dubow, J.S., & Childs, N.M. (1998). New Coca-Cola, mixture perception, and the flavor balance hypothesis. *Journal of Business Research*, 43 (3), 147-155.

Fey, C.F., & Beamish, P.W. (2000). Joint venture conflict: the case of Russian international joint ventures. *International Business Review*, 9 (2), 139-162.

Frazier, G., Gill, J.D., & Kale, S.H. (1989). Dealer dependence levels and reciprocal actions in a channel of distribution in a developing country. *Journal of Marketing*, 53 (Winter), 50-69.

Ger, G., & Belk, R.W. (1996). I'd like to buy the world a Coca-Cola: consumptionscapes of the "less affluent world". *Journal of Consumer Policy*, 19 (3), 271-304.

Glowacki, R. (1991). State of the market structure and its implications. *International Studies of Management and Organization*, 21, 39-58.

Green, D.H., Barclay, P.W., & Ryan, A.B. (1995). Entry strategy and long term performance: Conceptualization & Empirical Examination. *Journal of Marketing*, 59 (October), 1-16.

Hare, P. (1993). Economic prospects in Hungary: the rise of the private sector. *Business Strategy Review*, 4 (2), 39-57.

Hill, C.W.L., Hwang, P., & Kim, W.C. (1990). An eclectic theory of the choice of international entry mode. *Strategic Management Journal*, 11, 117-128.

Holey, G., Cox, T., Shipley, D., Fahy, J., Beracs, J., & Kolos, K. (1996). Foreign direct investment in Hungary: resource acquisition and domestic competitive advantage. *Journal of Business Studies*, 27 (4), 683-709.

Hymer, S.H. (1960). *The international operations of national firms: a study of direct foreign investment*. Cambridge, MA: MIT Press.

Kim, W., & Hwang, P. (1992) Global strategy and multinationals' entry mode choice. *Journal of International Business Studies*, 23 (1), 29-53.

Kindleberger, C. (1969). *American business abroad*. New Haven, NY: Yale University Press.

Klein, S., & Roth, V.J. (1990). A transaction cost analysis model of channel integration in international markets. *Journal of Marketing Research*, 27 (May), 196-208.

Kornai, J. (1980). *Economics of shortage*. New York, NY: North-Holland.

Kumar, K., & Subramaniam, V. (1997). A contingency framework for the mode of entry decision. *Journal of World Business*, 32 (1), 53-72.

Kvint, V. (1994). Don't give up on Russia. *Harvard Business Review*, (March-April), 62-74.

Larimo, J. (1995). The foreign direct investment decision process: case studies of different types of decision processes in Finnish firms. *Journal of Business Research*, 33 (1), 25-55.

Lessard, D.R. (1974). International diversification and foreign direct investment. In D. Eiteman & A. Stonehill (eds.), *Multinational business finance*, Reading, MA: Addison Wesley.

Marinov, M., Cox, T., Avlonitis, G., & Kouremenos, T. (1993). Marketing approaches in Bulgaria. *European Journal of Marketing*, 27 (11/12), 35-46.

McCarthy, D.J., & Puffer, S.M. (1997). Strategic flexibility for MNE success in Russia: evolving beyond entry modes. *Journal of World Business*, 32 (4), 293-319.

McCarthy, D.J., Puffer, S.M., & Simmonds, P.J. (1993). Riding the Russian roller coaster: US firms' recent experience and future plans in the former USSR. *California Management Review*, 36 (1), 99-115.

MacDougall, G.D. (1960). The benefits and costs of private investment from abroad: a theoretical approach. *Economic Record*, 33, 13-35.

Mascarenhas, B. (1982). Coping with uncertainty in international business. *Journal of International Business Studies*, 13 (3), 87-98.

Melin, L. (1992). Internationalization as a strategy process: *Strategic Management Journal*, 13, 99-118.

Mueller, R.D., Wenthe, J., & Baron, P. (1993). Case note: the evolution of distribution systems. *International Marketing Review*, 10 (4), 36-52.

Nakata, C., & Sivakumar, K. (1997). Emerging market conditions and their impact on first mover advantages: an integrative review. *International Marketing Review*, 14 (6), 461-485.

Nath, D. (1998). Organizational responses to a hypercompetitive environment: a case study of Pepsi Canada. *Journal of Business Research*, 41, 41-48.

Nigh, D., Walters, P., & Kuhlman, J.A. (1990). US-USSR joint ventures: an examination of the early entrants. *Columbia Journal of World Business*, 25, 20-27.

Oram, R. (1996). Consumerism's new citadel: western companies are pouring into Russia to meet the rapidly increasing demand for consumer goods. *Financial Times*, July 31, 19.

Randall, L.M., & Coakley, L.A. (1998). Building successful partnerships in Russia and Belarus: the impact of culture on strategy. *Business Horizons*, 41 (2), 15-22.

Raphael, T. (1998). Don't look to Moscow for Russian reform. *Wall Street Journal*, August 18, 6.

Reddy, A.C. (1991). The role of marketing in the economic development of Eastern European countries. *Journal of Applied Business Research*, 7 (3), 104-109.

Reinganum, J., & Helsell, T. (1994). To market, to market. *The China Business Review*, 21 (1), 30-34.

Robinson, A. (1996). Russia comes in from the cold: commerce rather than strategic considerations increasingly govern relationships in the former Soviet bloc. *Financial Times*, July 23, 17.

Samiee, S. (1993). Retailing and channel considerations in developing countries: a review and research propositions. *Journal of Business Research*, 27, 103-130.

Shama, A., & Merrell, M.N. (1997). Russia's true business performance: inviting to international business? *Journal of World Business*, 32 (4), 320-332.

Shama, A. (1992). Transforming the consumer in Russia and Eastern Europe. *International Marketing Review*, 9 (2), 43-59.

Shama, A. (1994). Transformation of marketing management in Russia: a qualitative and theory building approach. *The International Executive*, 36 (5), 599-624.

Slater, J. (1996). Foreign direct investment in the transition to a market economy. In P. Artisien-Maksimenko & Y. Abjubei (eds.), *Foreign investment in Russia and other Soviet successor states* (pp. 3-23). New York, NY: St. Martin's Press.

Snavely, W.B., Miassoedov, S., & McNeilly, K. (1998). Cross-cultural peculiarities of the Russian entrepreneur: adapting to the new Russians. *Business Horizons*, 41 (2), 8-14.

Thornhill, J. (1999) Should we support Primakov? *Financial Times*, March, 23 25.

Tourevski, M., & Morgan, E. (1993). *Cutting the red tape: how western companies can profit in the new Russia.* New York, NY: Free Press.

Vernon, R. (1966). International investment and international trade in the product cycle. *Quarterly Journal of Economics*, 80, 190-207.

Wright, M., Filatotchev, I., & Buck, T. (1993). The role of buy-outs in restructuring Central and Eastern Europe. *International Business Review*, 2 (3), 239-252.

Zurawicki, L., & Becker, K. (1994). Marketing issues and strategies for change in Central/Eastern European & CIS countries. *Journal of Euromarketing*, 3 (2), 61-90.

American Software Firms in Europe: Acquire, Invest or Partner?

Rod McNaughton

SUMMARY. This paper focuses on the antecedents of the form of inter-organisational governance used by U.S. software firms in their relationships with European firms. Specifically, whether the choice between acquisition, investment (joint venture or equity exchange) or contractual agreement is associated with characteristics such as the host country, industrial sector, range of functions covered by the relationship, technological intensity, or year in which the relationship occurred. The influence of these antecedents is investigated using data on 682 relationships between U.S. and European software firms that occurred between 1985 and 1995. The analysis shows that choice of a contractual agreement is almost exclusive, but the relative likelihood of an acquisition or an investment is increased when a relationship involves a larger number of functions. The likelihood of an acquisition is decreased if the European partner is located outside of the U.K., but the likelihood of an investment is increased. Finally, industrial sector, technological intensity and year do not have a significant influence on the choice of alliance form. Possible explanations for these results and their implications for research and managerial practice are discussed. *[Article copies available for a fee from The Haworth Document Delivery Service: 1-800-342-9678.*

Rod McNaughton is Professor, Department of Marketing, University of Otago, Corner of Union and Clyde Streets, P.O. Box 56, Dunedin, NZ (E-mail: rmcnaughton@commerce.otago.ac.nz).

[Haworth co-indexing entry note]: "American Software Firms in Europe: Acquire, Invest or Partner?" McNaughton, Rod. Co-published simultaneously in *Journal of Euromarketing* (International Business Press, an imprint of The Haworth Press, Inc.) Vol. 10, No. 1, 2001, pp. 49-70; and: *Foreign Direct Investment and Strategic Alliances in Europe* (ed: Hong Liu) International Business Press, an imprint of The Haworth Press, Inc., 2001, pp. 49-70. Single or multiple copies of this article are available for a fee from The Haworth Document Delivery Service [1-800-342-9678, 9:00 a.m. - 5:00 p.m. (EST). E-mail address: getinfo@haworthpressinc.com].

KEYWORDS. Strategic alliance, acquisition, joint venture, foreign investment, software firms, Europe

INTRODUCTION

The form used to govern inter-organisational relationships attracts considerable attention from both academics and managers. It is an area of management decision-making that occurs at the interface between the ownership boundaries of a firm and its environment. In essence it involves a strategic decision about the balance between co-operation and control, and between the costs and benefits of ownership. This paper investigates the antecedents of these decisions, specifically, whether the host country, industrial sector, technological intensity, number of functions, or year influences the choice between acquisition, investment (joint venture or equity exchange), or contractual agreement. (The term "alliance" is used throughout the paper when these three forms are referred to collectively.) The form of 682 international alliances with European firms is analysed covering the period 1985 to 1995.

Recent business rhetoric and management practice has influenced understanding of the weights in the balance of co-operation and control. The benefits of co-operating through various forms of contractual agreement to accomplish a common goal are now emphasised (Terpstra and Somonin, 1993). These "strategic alliances" are seen as a possible response to shorter product-life-cycles and increased costs of research and development (Gupta, 1991; Badaracco, 1991), to a need for new or cheaper resources (Ohmae, 1989), or as a means to enter foreign markets quickly (Potts and Behr, 1987; Lewis, 1990). While alliances are still a minor part of overall strategy in some sectors, and rates of alliance formation are generally slowing, the software industry is singularly prolific in its level of alliance activity (Hagedoorn and Schakenraad, 1992).

It is important to understand how various antecedent conditions influence the choice between alternative ways of governing a relationship as the choice of form is ultimately linked to performance. As a consequence, there is a cohesive stream of academic research that investigates the choice of strategic alliance form. Examples include Sengupta and Perry (1997), Hagedoorn and Narula (1996), Garcia-Canal (1996), and Contractor and Kundu (1998), among many others. This paper enhances understanding of the choice of form by investigating:

- the use of both equity investment and acquisition against the backdrop of a preponderance of contractual alliances, and
- the choice of alliance form in a particular sector, and over an extended time period.

The analyses in this paper are not unique in either regard, although the bulk of the literature does not address acquisitions, and investigates a cross-section of industries (Contractor and Kundu, 1998, 326). The focus on U.S. international alliances with European firms provides a description of the important linkages that are developing between the software industries in two of the Triad regions. Europe is an important host for the international activities of American software firms. By considering both contractual agreements and acquisitions, this paper links "strategic alliances" to foreign direct investment, emphasising the important theme of this volume.

This paper is organised as follows: The motives for relationship formation in the software industry are briefly reviewed. The forms of alliances are then described. Hypotheses are formulated about the potential influence of antecedent conditions on the choice of form. A description of the data and the results of statistical tests follow this. Finally, the paper concludes with observations about the implications of the findings for both further academic study and management practice.

MOTIVES FOR ALLIANCES IN THE SOFTWARE INDUSTRY

The range of motives for alliance formation has been widely studied and need not be reiterated in detail. Excellent reviews and integrative models are available in Cecil, Green and McNaughton (1996), and in Varadarajan and Cunningham (1995). The broad conclusion of these reviews is that alliances of various forms are motivated by the desire to reduce the uncertainty associated with accessing new or extra-regional markets, resources for production, technical innovations, or methods of reducing operating costs. The propensity of firms to enter strategic alliances is influenced by a set of firm characteristics, industry characteristics, and environmental characteristics. (See Varadadajan and Cunningham, 1995 for a list of these characteristics.)

The specific rationales for alliances involving software developers have attracted particular attention, partly because of the proclivity for alliances in this sector. Hagedoorn and Schakenraad (1992), for example, attribute the high rate of alliance formation to the crucial role software plays in linking sub-fields of information technologies, and the natural complement of computer hardware and software firms. Computer hardware manufacturers often lack specialised R&D capabilities that can be provided by independent software firms, and many independent software firms lack the financial resources of established hardware firms.

Rao and Klein (1994) attribute the importance of alliances in the sector to the lack of marketing-assets among new software firms that seek relationships with established firms to commercialise and market their developments. Further, they suggest that because software firms often have difficulties fully appropriating the benefits of their research, relationships tend to be collaborative rather than arms-length.

Another argument is that software alliances are essentially customer driven (Kulkosky, 1989; Arend, 1991). Purchasers of high technology are sophisticated users that demand integrated "enterprise solutions" that test the limits of even the largest computer and software vendors (Dunn, Friar and Thomas, 1991). As one industry observer noted: "Computers are being adopted in so many industries for so many reasons that we couldn't cover it all properly without alliances" (*The Financial Post,* 1990, 37). Moreover, buyers are refusing to integrate systems internally and are shifting this role to outside parties. This forces vendors to seek alliances with several, sometimes dozens, of other firms to put together a complete solution (Kulkosky 1989).

ALLIANCE FORM

Given strong motives for alliance formation, the question turns to the form alliances can take, and the relative frequencies with which they are used. Alliances can take many forms. A salient distinction is between those that involve an equity commitment and those that do not (Baranson, 1990; Gulati, 1995). Equity based alliance agreements specify finite financial investments, management structures, and profit sharing arrangements. Equity alliances are assumed to be more strategic and long term (Osborn and Baughn, 1990). Non-equity agreements typically cover basic objectives, resource commitments, and operating mechanisms. Examples include marketing, distribution and R&D agreements. Such agreements are supposed to be characterised by mutual trust, co-operative decision-making and limited life spans.

The most frequently investigated form of equity alliance is the joint venture. In this form, two (or more) firms take an equity stake in the formation of a third new firm. However, equity exchanges serve a similar purpose and can be considered as a direct alternative to a joint venture, especially in the case of only two partners (Garcia-Canal, 1996). In the analyses reported here, joint ventures are combined with equity exchanges and are called "investments."

A final form of equity "alliance" is the merger or acquisition. (Mergers are not distinguished from acquisitions for the purposes of this research, and both are simply referred to as "acquisitions.") Considering an acquisition to be a form of strategic alliance is controversial. Some researchers argue for a broad definition of alliances that includes acquisitions (e.g., Hakansson, Kjellberg and Lundgren, 1993; Gantz, 1990; Borys and Jemison, 1989), while other disagree. An obvious difference is that acquisitions always affect ownership structures. However, Bleeke and Ernst (1993) found that 75% of alliances between small and large firms end with the purchase of the small firm by its larger partner. At least some contractual alliances may, therefore, be regarded as precursors to take-over (Bleeke and Ernst, 1993), or at least as a testing ground for potential acquisitions (Ahern, 1991; Doz, 1991). The argument for characterising acquisitions as an alternative to investments or contractual agreements is particularly strong in the software sector where acquisitions are rarely hostile. This is because the corporate assets of software firms are integrally linked to the human capital of particular individuals within the firm, and a hostile take-over could cause valuable people to leave the acquired firm.

A large number of empirical studies report the relative frequency of alliance forms, and in particular, compare the use of joint ventures with non-equity contractual agreements. The general finding is that non-equity agreements are more frequent, though there is considerable variation between both industries and years. The following are illustrative results from studies that include alliances between U.S. and European firms:

- Sengupta and Perry (1997) found that across IT sectors 78.4% of U.S.-European alliances completed in 1989 were contract agreements, and the remainder were joint ventures.
- Terpstra and Simonin (1993) found that for the period 1983-1987, 32% of alliances (across all industrial sectors) in the U.S. were

contractual agreements, 40% equity investments, 20% joint ventures, and 8% consortia. For the same time period, the percentages among European firms were 29% contractual agreements, 33% equity investments, 25% joint ventures, and 13% consortia.
- Murray (1995) found that for the period 1989-1992 alliances between U.S. based and European firms were: 39% contractual agreements, 7.4% equity investments, 42.7% joint ventures, and 11% consortia.

There are a large number of potentially influential antecedents to the choice of alliance form, both internal and external to the firm. However, syntheses of the alliance literature suggest that the essence of an alliance can be captured by a limited number of observable dimensions. Vyas, Shelburn, and Rogers (1995) summarise these dimensions:

- Sector–intra-industry versus inter-industry.
- Arena–domestic versus international.
- Relationship–supplier versus non-supplier.
- Technology–market, state and fusion.

Similarly, Varadarajan and Cunningham (1995) identify three dimensions: geographic scope, industry scope, and functional scope. The last of these can be interpreted as a combination of Vyas et al.'s relationship and technology dimensions resulting in a list of specific alliance types. Varadarajan and Cunningham (1995) also suggest that an alternative measure of the functional scope of an alliance is provided by the number of activities in the value chain encompassed by the alliance (i.e., whether firms in an alliance co-operate on one or more activities). This measure is used in the analyses reported in this paper.

The importance of these dimensions is illustrated by their repeated use in empirical studies, and frequent statistically significant relationship with alliance form (e.g., Hagedoorn, 1993; Terpstra and Simonin, 1993; Murray, 1995; Sengupta and Perry, 1997; Garcia-Canal, 1996). Each of these dimensions has an influence on the uncertainties experienced by a firm. Geographic scope has implications for uncertainty about the behaviour of partners and about country specific demand. Sector scope has implications for uncertainty about technological change and competitor behaviour. Functional scope influences the extent to which a firm is exposed to its partner, and uncertainty about demand. Thus, if alliances are formed primarily to mitigate uncertainty, the form that is chosen should reflect the primary source of that uncertainty.

HYPOTHESES ABOUT CHOICE OF ALLIANCE FORM

Three theoretical approaches are commonly used to link antecedents to the choice of alliance form (Kogut, 1988): transaction cost theory, strategic behaviour, and organisational learning. Each of these addresses a fairly narrow set of rationales. As the analyses presented in this paper concern very broad antecedent dimensions, an appropriate framework is also necessarily broad. Thus, the syncretic (or eclectic) approach advocated by Contractor (1990), Contractor and Kundu (1998), and Hill, Hwang and Kim (1990) offers a relevant framework here. The arguments developed below about the influence of antecedents on alliance form draw on the eclectic spirit of this framework.

Geographic Scope

Alliances with foreign firms are a means to quickly enter new markets, take advantage of an existing distribution system and local knowledge, or to meet local participation requirements (e.g., Porter, 1986; Morris and Hergert, 1987; Harrigan, 1987; Potts and Behr, 1987; Ohmae, 1989; and Lewis, 1990). Uncertainties arise about partner behaviour because of different norms, culture and business practices, and about demand because of changing consumer preferences or an unstable political or economic environment (Kogut, 1988). Behavioural uncertainty combined with physical and organisational distance can make it difficult to monitor and assess the performance of a partner. Demand uncertainty requires organisational structures that can quickly adapt to a changing environment. Thus, some authors recommend that the more uncertain the environment, the more appropriate a structured mechanism (usually a joint venture) that provides high access to information and some ownership control (e.g., Kogut, 1988; Parkhe, 1991). Overexposure through acquisition is cautioned though, primarily because of the financial risk, and difficulty incorporating local knowledge (Contractor and Kundu, 1998, 339).

In the case of U.S. software firms allying with European partners, contractual forms may dominate because of their flexibility, lower financial risk and operating costs. Acquisitions should be rare, but the likelihood of investments (joint ventures) should increase in the presence of greater behavioural or demand uncertainty. The U.K. is host to the largest proportion of alliances between U.S. and European software firms (49% in the data described later in this paper), and is the least culturally distant on the Kogut-Singh index (1988). It is also the largest European market for English language software. Thus, relative to alliances with firms in the U.K., uncertainty is likely to be greater, and the following country specific effects on the choice of alliance form are expected:

- H_1: The likelihood that an alliance takes the form of an acquisition is decreased when the alliance is with a firm in a country other than the U.K.
- H_2: The likelihood that an alliance takes the form of an investment is increased when the alliance is with a firm in a country other than the U.K.

Industry Scope

Alliances may be formed between firms in different sectors, or with firms in the same sector. Co-operation with firms in different sectors has many advantages. Firms may use alliances to form backward linkages to strengthen their access to needed inputs, or they may form forward linkages to gain access to markets, facilitating "quasi-vertical integration" (Anderson, 1992). Contractual alliances allow firms to benefit from increased specialisation while retaining many of the advantages of vertical integration (Leborgne and Lipietz, 1988), and can generate economies of scope (Walker, 1988; Cooke, 1988). A particularly common motive for inter-sectoral alliances is the development or transfer of new technology. Contractual alliances can open the door to a portfolio of new technologies, which can be explored at relatively low cost, and with low exit barriers. (See the discussion of technological intensity below.)

Alliances may also be formed between firms in the same industry that target essentially the same markets (Morris and Hergert, 1987). Anderson (1992) refers to these alliances as "quasi-horizontal" integration. Burgers, Hill and Kim (1993) provide two rationales for the creation of these alliances. First, they argue that firms will enter into alliances with competitors in order to reduce the uncertainty associated with unpredictable changes in consumer purchasing patterns. Second, alliances with competitors help firms to reduce the uncertainty created when their competitive actions have an effect on the market position of rivals. This competitive uncertainty exists because firms are not able to predict if rivals will initiate competitive moves, or if rivals will retaliate against competitive actions (Contractor and Lorange, 1988). Thus, intra-sector alliances generally involve situations where stronger relationships dampen uncertainty, and indeed where "lock-in" may be desirable. Thus, there are pressures that increase the likelihood of both investments and acquisitions among partners in the same sector.

The hypotheses about the effect of industrial scope on choice of alliance form are:

- H_3: The likelihood that an alliance takes the form of an acquisition is increased when the alliance is between firms in the same industrial sector.
- H_4: The likelihood that an alliance takes the form of an investment is increased when the alliance is between firms in the same industrial sector.

Functional Scope

A key definition of a "strategic" alliance is that it is formed to achieve a particular goal or set of goals. The objective(s) of the partnership, then, largely determine the functional scope of the relationship. These may relate to upstream activities (assessing new resources or R&D), the manufacturing or service delivery process itself, or downstream activities (marketing or distribution). For each step in the value chain, or number of projects at a particular step, that a firm shares with a partner, additional uncertainty is created. The source is primarily behavioural–partners may expropriate know-how, they may under-perform in some way, or they may withdraw leaving their role difficult to replace. A larger number of shared functions also imply complexity of organisation. Thus, as the number of functions involved in an alliance increases, there is greater pressure to employ either the stronger monitoring mechanisms of investment, or the hierarchical control provided by acquisitions.

The hypotheses relating choice of alliance form to functional scope is:

- H_5: The likelihood that an alliance takes the form of an acquisition increases with the number of functions to be shared by the partners.
- H_6: The likelihood that an alliance takes the form of an investment increases with the number of functions to be shared by the partners.

Technological Intensity

A number of studies have investigated a link between alliance form and technological intensity. (This literature is reviewed by Osborn and Baughan, 1990.) The observation is generally that contractual agreements and even informal collaboration occur with greater frequency in sectors where the technological state-of-the-art is uncertain (Hagedoorn, 1993). The logic that explains this pattern is that in technologically intense industries, firms experience uncertainty about the future path of technology. A series of contractual agreements offer a way to "hedge their bets," keeping informed and developing a number of alternative paths. If a particular path becomes an obvious dead-end, termination costs are low. Similarly, if a path looks particularly promising, a relationship already exists that can be built upon with further commitment and investment. Thus:

- H_7: The likelihood that an alliance takes the form of an acquisition decreases with the technological intensity of the alliance.
- H_8: The likelihood that an alliance takes the form of an investment decreases with the technological intensity of the alliance.

Year

The data analysed in this study cover the period 1985-1995. During this time, at least two environmental conditions have changed that could affect the choice of alliance form. First, business rhetoric shifted. The acceptance of contractual agreements, and knowledge about how to structure them increased during the period, potentially favouring this choice. Second, Single Europe was implemented. Related changes in legislation might have favoured international acquisitions earlier in the period, and investments and contractual agreements later in the period (Murray and Mahon, 1993). This variable is included as a control because of the potential effect of calibrating a single model from data that span an eleven-year period. (The frequency of alliance forms is shown by year in Figure 1.)

DATA

Alliances can be difficult to identify as they usually do not result in changes of ownership and are not scrutinised or recorded by a regula-

FIGURE 1. Alliances Between U.S. and European Software Firms 1985-1995

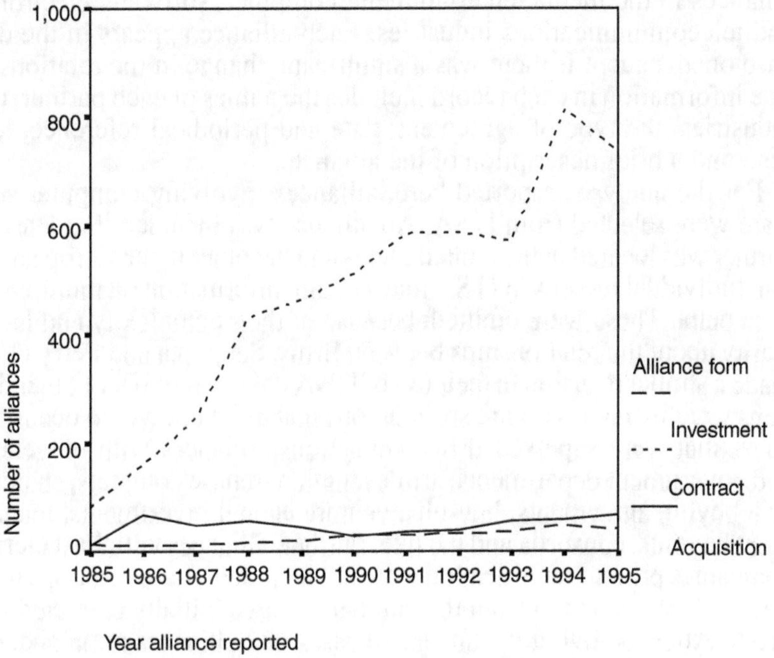

tory body. As a result, studies that examine relationships across a large number of alliances usually rely on reports of alliances in the business and trade press. An influential example of this approach is the Co-operative Agreements and Technology Indicators (CATI) database created by Hagedoorn and Schakenraad (1990, 1992) and their colleagues. This database contains information on over 10,000 co-operative agreements involving more than 4,000 firms in the IT sector. Other researchers have developed similar but less extensive listings (e.g., Ghemawat, Porter, and Rawlinson, 1986; Morris and Hergert, 1987; Ellram, 1992; Anderson 1992, 1993; and Hakansson, Kjellberg and Lundgren, 1993; Murray, 1995).

The alliances analysed for this paper were identified in a similar way, using the "Information Technology Strategic Alliances Database" (ITSA) database marketed by Itsunami Inc. of Berkeley, California. ITSA tracked alliances using a variety of North American trade journals and business periodicals until its termination in 1996. At the end of 1995 it covered eleven years and contained descriptions of over 30,000 alliances in the media, entertainment, computer, software, electronics, and telecommunications industries. Each alliance appears in the database once, except if there was a significant change in the relationship. The information in each record includes the names of each partner, their industries, the type of agreement, date and periodical reference, location, and a brief description of the alliance.

For the analyses reported here, alliances involving computer software were selected from ITSA. An alliance was included if at least one partner was located in the United States and the other in the European Union. Individual records in ITSA may contain information on multiple alliance pairs. These were omitted, because of their complexity and lack of clarity about the relationships between firms. Sengupta and Perry (1997) made a similar decision in their use of ITSA data. A number of other deletions were made, involving speculations that alliances would occur, alliances that were superseded by acquisitions, alliances with universities and government departments, arm's length purchase contracts, standards or lobbying agreements, lawsuits, venture capital investments, management buyouts, consortia and the like. Further, alliances with East German companies prior to reunification were not included These deletions represent an 18% reduction from the number of cases initially extracted from ITSA. After removing the unwanted cases 682 alliances remained. (For comparison, the same procedure identified 5,348 alliances where both partners are located in the U.S.)

Slightly more than one third of the alliances were reported in *Computer World*, and slightly less than a third in *The Wall Street Journal.* The remaining cases were reported in numerous periodicals. The most frequent U.S. based partners were Microsoft, IBM, and Oracle (accounting for about 3%, 3% and 2% of the cases). The most frequent partners in Europe were Siemans, Olivetti, ICL Plc., and Bull Groupe (accounting for about 2%, 2%, 1% and 1% of the cases respectively).

The use of media reports to identify alliances has numerous limitations (Hagedoorn and Schakenraad, 1992). First, there is a bias toward alliances that are "newsworthy" (often because they involve large well-known firms). Second, alliances are not always reported when they happen, or the reported alliance may fail to form. Similarly, alliance deaths are less likely to be reported than are births, so those that are ongoing, and those that were terminated must be treated with equal weight. Finally, there is little consistency in what information is reported. Some of these problems can be mitigated by gathering alliance information from a large number of sources, cross-checking between sources and standardising the collection and recording process (all of which are done by ITSA). A sample of the original references was consulted to check the accuracy of the records, and to aid further classification of the alliance characteristics.

VARIABLES

A combination of manual and automated procedures were used to code six variables:

- Alliance forms. The dependent variable has three possible values: (0) contractual agreement, (1) equity swap or joint venture, and (2) acquisition.
- Geographic scope. This variable is operationalised as the country in which the European partner is located: (0) United Kingdom, (1) France, (2) Germany, and (3) another country in the European Union. Location was determined by the locus of the alliance, not the headquarters location of the ultimate owner. Geographic scope is treated as a unique property of a country, which includes both sources of behavioural uncertainty (such as cultural distance from the U.S.), and sources of demand uncertainty (such as market size, or political risk). The U.K., France or Germany is home to 80% of the European alliance partners.
- Sector. This variable has two values: (0) if partners are both in the same sector, and (1) otherwise. While the alliances all concern software, the participating firms are not necessarily software developers (or may not be the software division of a large diversified firm). ITSA uses a twelve-category scheme to classify the primary business interest of each alliance participant (firm or division of a large firm). These categories were compared for the partners in an alliance.
- Number of functions. ITSA uses a series of symbols to indicate the activities to be jointly undertaken in an alliance. A variable was created that is a count of the number of business functions reported to be covered by the alliance (e.g., an agreement to co-operate on marketing and production = 2).
- Technological intensity. This variable is the industry rank (1-5) based on average R&D as a percentage of sales reported in the annual *Business Week R&D Scoreboard*. This follows the approach used by Sengupta and Perry (1997).
- Year. The year in which the alliance was reported.

The number of functions, technological intensity and year are treated as continuous variables. This attributes to them a higher level of measurement sophistication than is strictly true given the limited range of values that they can assume. However, this is necessitated by the need to reduce the number of parameters estimated in the polychotomous logistic regression model reported below as the imbalance between alliance forms creates a number of empty cells in the covariate patterns. Bivariate tests (not shown) suggest that treating them as continuous rather than ordinal or nominal variables does not alter the general conclusion about their relationship to alliance form.

RESULTS

Table 1 shows alliance forms cross-tabulated with each of the independent variables. There is an imbalance between frequency of choice between acquisitions (9%), investments (8%), and contractual agreements (83%). Alliances are most common between firms in different sectors (75%), involve co-operation on about two functions, and are technologically intensive. Chi-Square or F-tests for significant differences between alliance forms were calculated. These show that alliance form is significantly associated with the host country, number of functions, and technological intensity. Examination of the Chi-Square residuals and group means reveal:

- Acquisitions are more common in the U.K. than would be expected if form and host country were independent.
- Investments are more common in France and "other" European countries than would otherwise be expected.
- There are fewer contractual agreements in the U.K. than expected.
- There are more acquisitions between firms in the same sector than expected.
- Contractual agreements involve significantly fewer functions.
- Investments involve significantly higher technological intensity.

To provide a holistic view of the relationships between the antecedent variables and alliance form, a polychotomous (multinomial) logistic regression model was calibrated. The results are presented in Table 2. The primary benefits of this analysis over the bivariate analyses are that it provides a measure of the relative strength of association between the

TABLE 1. Frequency of Alliances by Form and Antecedent Variables

	Acquisition	Investment	Contract	Total
Location of partner (count)				
• U.K.	43	23	271	330
• France	9	8	94	111
• Germany	5	4	99	108
• Other	4	18	104	133
• Total	61	53	568	682
$\chi^2 = 23.4$ p = 0.001				
Sector (count)				
• Same sector	18	17	137	172
• Different	43	36	431	510
$\chi^2 = 2.3$ p = 0.320				
Number of functions (mean)	2.0	2.0	1.2	1.7
F = 1,070.9 p = 0.000				
Technological intensity (mean)	3.0	3.7	3.1	3.2
F = 3.4 p = 0.033				
Year (mean)	1991	1991	1991	1991
F = 0.5 p = 0.613				

TABLE 2. Polychotomous Logistic Regression Model of Choice of Alliance

	Acquisition	Investment	−2 Log-Likelihood
Location of partner			111.6
• U.K.	–	–	p = 0.041
• France	−0.30	0.24	
• Germany	−0.48	0.04	
• Other	−1.09	0.80	
Sector			102.7
• Same sector	0.48	−0.36	p = 0.380
• Different	–	–	
Number of functions	26.6	26.5	561.9 p = 0.000
Technological intensity	−0.15	0.19	104.9 p = 0.122
Year	−0.09	−0.14	101.2 p = 0.490
Intercept	−31.6	−27.5	100.7

Model fit: ρ = 0.699 $\chi^2 = 517.6$ p = 0.000

antecedents and alliance form, standardised parameters comparable across variables, and statistical control over covariates.

One caution is that the imbalance in cases between alliance forms (and indeed between the levels of antecedents as well) causes empty cells in the covariate patterns. This affects the validity of the parameter estimates, and despite the overall good fit of the model, the individual parameter estimates have large standard errors and few can be statistically distinguished from zero. A second problem is that there is some aliasing among the antecedent variables, particularly between location and sector, and sector and technology intensity, but this interaction is within the usually accepted limits. Despite these difficulties, the model parameters can be usefully interpreted as a standardised description of the relationships in these data. (The rationale for this conclusion is discussed in detail below.)

The model parameters are estimated relative to the choice of a contractual agreement, and for location and sector relative to the U.K., and both partners being in a different sector. Positive parameters indicate that the variable increases the likelihood of an acquisition or investment relative to a contract. Negative parameters indicate the reverse. The greatest reduction in the overall log-likelihood is brought about by the number of functions involved in the alliance followed by the location of the partner. The pattern of individual parameters generally coincides with the observations made from the residuals and group means, except that technological intensity is not a significant influence on choice. The large negative intercepts indicate the low probability of acquisitions and investments relative to contractual agreements.

DISCUSSION

The results of the analyses of alliances formed by software firms are generally in line with expectations from the eclectic framework, although relatively few significant relationships were found. With the exception of the number of functions involved, and to a lesser extent the location of the partner, broad antecedent dimensions do not strongly distinguish between the alliance forms. Two situations were identified where the pressures of uncertainty significantly increase the likelihood of an investment. Namely (1) when the alliance partner is located outside of the U.K. (and especially if it is also outside of France or Germany) (H_2), and (2) a larger number of functions are involved (H_6). Relative to the choice of a contractual agreement, the likelihood of an acquisition was found to decrease when the alliance partner is located outside of the U.K. (H_1), and to increase as a larger number of functions are involved (H_5). The valences of individual parameter estimates are all consistent with expectations, but cannot be distinguished statistically from zero. Thus, there is no statistical support for H_3, H_4, H_7 or H_8.

Problems with the number of empty covariate cells, and resulting large standard errors for parameters, suggest that these results should not be generalised to a larger population. This is a significant limitation, and disappointing. However, such caution may also be unwarranted. These results are based on a relatively large sample, and are essentially the population of "newsworthy" alliances that occurred during the time period. From this point of view, the empty covariate cells are structural, occurring for substantive reasons, not simply because of inadequate sample size (i.e., they represent combinations of alliance form and antecedents that do not occur). The import of this interpretation is that the results are genuine: in the software sector occurrences of non-contractual forms are rare and unique, and the influence of broad antecedents on the choice of these forms is small.

Some evidence in support of this position is gained by comparing the occurrence of alliance forms in these data with those analysed by Sengupta and Perry (1997). Sengupta and Perry used the ITSA data for all IT sectors to analyse alliances that occurred in 1989. Their data included 33 (10%) joint ventures and 295 (90%) contractual agreements between U.S. firms, and 16 (22%) joint ventures and 58 (78%) contractual agreements between U.S. and European firms. The percentage of joint ventures in both U.S.-U.S., and U.S.-European alliances between software firms alone is 4% for the same year (96% are contractual agreements). Clearly, investments are much less common in the software industry than in IT sectors as a whole.

A second related point is that both the frequency of partnering, and the use of alliance modes is closely associated with the strategies pursued by particular firms. For example, about 3% of DEC's alliances are equity based, while 47% of Computer Associates International's alliances are acquisitions (the result of an aggressive strategy to acquire independent software developers). Interestingly, the firms that are most active in forming alliances overall (by frequency of occurrence in the ITSA database) are below average with respect to the percentage of their alliances that are formed with European firms. One reason for this is that the top firms are multinational corporations with established overseas sales offices and sometimes research and production facilities as well (e.g., Microsoft's investments in Ireland). These subsidiaries enter into their own alliances, which do not appear as international given the definition of location used in these data. Further, those that do appear are more likely to be acquisitions or investments as these are more likely to involve the U.S. head office.

CONCLUSIONS

The primary message from these results is that the pressures generated by different sources of uncertainty are not generally strong enough in the software industry to influence firms to ally through investment or acquisition. The need for flexibility, exploration of a range of technological alternatives, and ease of exit dominate. The primary exception is the risk associated with exposing numerous business functions to a partner. When a relationship involves numerous functions, and therefore is supposed to be complex, the likelihood is much greater that a firm will seek greater structure and information through investment, or hierarchical control through acquisition. Second to this, but of less importance, is the location of the partner. For alliances with partners in Europe, location outside of the U.K. may generate sufficient demand and/or behavioural uncertainty to increase the likelihood of an investment. (It also reduces the likelihood of taking on the financial risk of an acquisition.)

The analyses reported in this paper are normative rather than prescriptive. The importance for managers, therefore, is primarily in terms of illustrating the collective trends in the industry. The results illustrate how firms typically respond to various types of uncertainty that are supposed to influence the choice of alliance form. Thus, a manager can assess their firm's overall strategy, or choice of form in a new alliance, in the context of general practice in the industry. In the absence of any information specific to a particular decision, the model could be used to choose a form for the alliance based on a few basic dimensions. The framework and findings sensitise managers to the potential importance of several broad influences on the choice of alliance form, but do little to offer advice for any one particular decision, which will be influenced by firm-specific considerations.

The contribution to theory, and implications for future research are more substantial. First this study is one of a few that explicitly include acquisition as an alternative form of partnering. The results suggest there is value in forging a stronger link between the strategic alliance and foreign direct investment literatures. This is underscored by the theme of this special issue, which combines papers on strategic alliances and foreign direct investment in the context of Europe. An obvious extension in the international arena is to situations where a suitable partner or alliance structure can not be identified, and green field investment becomes an option.

By focusing on the software sector, this study has illustrated one of the more extreme industry situations where in relative terms the choice contractual agreements is almost exclusive. The incidence of contractual co-operation is likely influenced by customer demand for enterprise solutions, and by the potential to lever both economies of scope and scale, rather than by the lack of pressures to make equity investments or acquisitions. That is, synergy is created by the flexibility and relatively low-cost of contractual agreements. Had this synergy not been recognised by firms in the industry, the current industrial organisation of the sector would be very different.

Most extant research on alliances is cross-industry, and thus compares the differing pressures toward or away from equity collaboration between sectors. (There are a few other studies specific sectors, for example, Contractor and Kundu's 1998 study of the hotel sector.) Studying a particular sector reduces the variability observed within broad dimensions such as technological intensity. Thus, future research should focus more on firm characteristics rather than on industry or environmental characteristics. One implication for future empirical studies is that observations from reports in business periodicals are insufficiently detailed. Finer detail is required about firm characteristics and strategies, preferably over time. While case study research is currently reported in the alliance literature, there is a need to balance this richer detail with observation of a sufficient number of cases to make useful generalisations.

REFERENCES

Ahern, R.D. 1991. *International Strategic Alliances: The Use of Cooperation by Canadian Firms.* Unpublished Ph.D. Dissertation, Department of Geography, University of Washington.

Anderson, M.J. 1992. *The Collaborative Edge: The Role of Collaborative Integration in the Organization and Locational Structure of Industry.* Unpublished PhD Dissertation, Department of Geography, Queen's University, Kingston, Ontario.

Anderson, M.J. 1993. "Collaborative Integration in the Canadian Pharmaceutical Industry" *Environment and Planning A* 25, 1815-1838.

Arend, M. 1991. "Tougher Customers Drive Vendor Alliances" *Wall Street Computer Review* 8 (8), 16-23.

Badaracco, J.L. 1991. *The Knowledge Link: How Firms Compete Through Strategic Alliances* (Harvard Business School Press, Boston).

Baranson, J. 1990. "Transnational Strategic Alliances: Why, What, Where and How" *Multinational Business* 2, 54-61.

Bleeke, J., and Ernst D. 1993. "The Way to Win in Cross Border Alliances," In J. Bleeke, and D. Ernst eds. *Collaborating to Compete: Using Strategic Alliances and Acquisition in the Global Marketplace*. New York: Wiley.

Borys, B., and Jemison D. 1989. "Hybrid Organizations as Strategic Alliances" *Academy of Management Review* 14 (2), 234-249.

Burgers, W.P., Hill, C.W.L., and Kim, W.C. 1993. "Theory of Global Strategic Alliances: The Case of the Global Auto Industry" *Strategic Management Journal* 14 (6), 419-432.

Cecil, B.P., Green, M.B., and McNaughton, R.B. 1996. "Patterns of Strategic Alliances Among Information Technology Firms in the United States" *Geografiska Annaler B* 3, 129-147.

Contractor, F.J. 1990. "Contractual and Cooperative Forms of International Business: Towards a Unified Theory of Modal Choice", *Management International Review*, 30, 31-54.

Contractor, F.J., and Kundu, S.K. 1998. "Modal Choice in a World of Alliances: Analysing Organisational Forms in the International Hotel Sector" *Journal of International Business Studies*, 29 (2), 325-358.

Cooke, P. 1988. "Flexible Integration, Scope Economies, and Strategic Alliances: Social and Spatial Mediations" *Environment and Planning D* 6, 281-300.

Doz, Y. 1988. "Technology Partnerships Between Larger and Smaller Firms: Some Critical Issues," In F. Contractor and P. Lorange eds. *Cooperative Strategies in International Business*. Lexington: Lexington Books.

Dunn, D.T., Friar, J.H., and Thomas, C.A. 1991. "An Approach to Selling High-Tech Solutions" *Industrial Marketing Management* 20, 149-159.

Ellram, L.M. 1992. "Patterns in International Alliances" *Journal of Business Logistics* 13 (1), 1-25.

Garcia-Canal, E. 1996. "Contractual Form in Domestic and International Strategic Alliances" *Organisational Studies* 17 (5), 773-794.

Gantz, J. 1990. "Strategic Alliances: How do they effect you?" *Network Management 8 (7), 74-78.*

Ghemawat, P., Porter, M.E., and Rawlinson, R. 1986. "Patterns of International Alliance Activity," In Porter, M.ed. *Competition in Global Industries*. Boston: Harvard Business School Press, 345-366.

Gulati, R. 1995. "Does Familiarity Breed Trust? The Implications of Repeated Ties for Contractual Choice in Alliances" *Academy of Management Journal* 38 (1), 85-112.

Gupta, A.K. 1991. "Improving R&D/Marketing Relations: R&D's Perspective" *Research and Development Management* 20 (4), 277-290.

Hagedoorn, J. 1993. "Understanding the Rationale of Strategic Technology Partnering: Interorganizational Modes of Cooperation and Sectoral Differences" *Strategic Management Journal* 14 (5), 371-385.

Hagedoorn, J., and Narula, R. 1996. "Choosing Organisational Modes of Strategic Technology Partnering: International and Sectoral Differences" *Journal of International Business Studies* 265-284.

Hagedoorn, J., and Schakenraad, J. 1992. "Leading Companies and Networks of Strategic Alliances in Information Technologies" *Research Policy* 21, 163-190.

Hakansson, P., Kjellberg, H., and Lundgren, A. 1993. "Strategic Alliances in Global Biotechnology=A Network Approach" *International Business Review* 2 (1), 65-82.

Harrigan, K.R. 1987. "Strategic Alliances: Their New Role in Global Competition" *Columbia Journal of World Business* 22 (2), 67-70.

Hill, C.W., Hwang, P., Kim, W.C. 1990. "An Eclectic Theory of the Choice of International Entry Mode" *Strategic Management Journal* 11, 117-128.

Kogut, B. 1988. "Joint Ventures: Theoretical and Empirical Perspectives" *Strategic Management Journal*, 9, 319-332.

Kogut, B., and Singh, H. 1988. "The Effect of National Culture on the Choice of Entry Mode" *Journal of International Business Studies* 19, 413-431.

Kulkosky, V. 1989. "Strategic Alliances Buoy New Technology Book" *Wall Street Computer Review* 6 (8), 19-24, 86.

Leborgne, D., and Lipietz, A. 1988. "New Technologies, new Modes of Regulation: Some Spatial Implications" *Environment and Planning D* 6, 263-280.

Lewis, J.D. 1990. *Partnerships for Profit: Structuring and Managing Strategic Alliances.* New York: The Free Press.

Morris, D., and Hergert, M. 1987. "Trends in International Collaborative Agreements" *Columbia Journal of World Business* 22 (2), 15-21.

Moxon, R., Roehl, T., and Truitt J. 1988. "International Cooperative Ventures in the Commercial Aircraft Industry: Gains, Sure, but what's my share?" In F. Contractor and P. Lorange eds. *Cooperative Strategies in International Business.* Lexington: Lexington Books.

Murray, J.Y. 1995. "Patterns in Domestic vs. International Strategic Alliances: An Investigation of U.S. Multinational Firms", *Multinational Business Review* 3 (2), 7-16.

Murray, E.A., and Mahon, J.F. 1993, "Strategic Alliances: Gateway to the New Europe?" *Long Range Planning* 26 (4), 102-111.

Ohmae, K. 1989. "The Global Logic of Strategic Alliances" *Harvard Business Review* March-April, 143-154.

Osborn, R.N., and Baughn, C.C., 1990. "Forms of Interorganizational Governance for Multinational Alliances" *Academy of Management Journal* 33(3), 503-519.

Parke, A. 1991. "Interfirm Diversity, Organisational Learning, and Longevity in Global Strategic Alliances" *Journal of International Business Studies* 22, 579-601.

Porter, M.E., and Fuller, M.B. 1986. "Coalitions and Global Strategy," In M. Porter ed. *Competition in Global Industries.* Boston: Harvard Business School Press.

Potts, M., and Behr, P. 1987. "Strange Global Bedfellows" *Across the Board* February, 24-30.

Rao, P.M., and Klein, J.A. 1994. "Growing Importance of Marketing Strategies for the Software Industry" *Industrial Marketing Management* 23, 29-37.

Sengupta, S., and Perry, M. 1997. "Some Antecedents of Global Strategic Alliance Formation" *Journal of International Marketing* 5 (1), 31-50.

Terpstra, V., and Simonin, B.L. 1993. "Strategic Alliances in the Triad, An Exploratory Study" *Journal of International Marketing* 1 (1), 4-25.

The Financial Post. 1990. "Strategic Alliances Wave of the Future" October 22, 37.

Varadarajan, P.R., and Cunningham, M.H. 1995. "Strategic Alliances: A Synthesis of Conceptual Foundations", *Journal of the Academy of Marketing Science*, 23 (4), 282-296.

Vyas, N.M., Shelburn, W.L., and Rogers, D.C. 1995. "An Analysis of Strategic Alliances: Forms, Functions and Framework" *Journal of Business and Industrial Marketing* 10 (3), 47-60.

Walker, G. 1988. "Strategic Sourcing, Vertical Integration, and Transaction Costs" *Interfaces* 18 (3), 62-73.

International Strategic Alliances: The Impact of Behavioral Characteristics on Success

Saleema Kauser
Vivienne Shaw

SUMMARY. This paper presents the findings of a study of 114 international strategic alliances between UK firms and their European, US and Japanese partners. The research aims to assess the influence of behavioral characteristics on the success of international strategic alliances. The findings show that high levels of co-ordination, commitment, trust and communications are good predictors of international partnership success. While conflict is present in international partnerships, it is found to hinder a good performance. *[Article copies available for a fee from The Haworth Document Delivery Service: 1-800-342-9678. E-mail address: <getinfo@haworthpressinc.com> Website: <http://www.HaworthPress.com> © 2001 by The Haworth Press, Inc. All rights reserved.]*

KEYWORDS. International strategic alliances, performance, behavioral characteristics

---

Saleema Kauser is Research Fellow, Executive Development Centre, Manchester Business School, Booth Street West, Manchester M15 6PB (Email: skauser@man.mbs.ac.uk). Vivienne Shaw is Associate Professor, Department of Marketing, University of Otago, P.O. Box 56, Dunedin, New Zealand (Email: vshaw@commerce.otago.ac.nz).

[Haworth co-indexing entry note]: "International Strategic Alliances: The Impact of Behavioral Characteristics on Success." Kauser, Saleema, and Vivienne Shaw. Co-published simultaneously in *Journal of Euromarketing* (International Business Press, an imprint of The Haworth Press, Inc.) Vol. 10, No. 1, 2001, pp. 71-98; and: *Foreign Direct Investment and Strategic Alliances in Europe* (ed: Hong Liu) International Business Press, an imprint of The Haworth Press, Inc., 2001, pp. 71-98. Single or multiple copies of this article are available for a fee from The Haworth Document Delivery Service [1-800-342-9678, 9:00 a.m. - 5:00 p.m. (EST). E-mail address: getinfo@haworthpressinc.com].

INTRODUCTION

Over the last two decades the world economy has been dramatically transformed. The business environment is characterized by increasing complexity, uncertainty and discontinuity. Changing market conditions, intensified global competition and increasingly shorter product life cycles mean that firms are having to re-examine the traditional methods and strategies for doing business (Ohmae 1989; Bartlett and Ghoshal 1987). Managers are realizing that, no matter how strong and resourceful their firms might be, they are no longer able to maintain a competitive advantage at every step in the value chain in all national markets, nor are they able to maintain a cutting edge in the wide range of technologies required for the design, development, manufacture and marketing of new products. Thus international strategic alliances have become an important means to rationalize operations to overcome potential difficulties and to help firms regain and maintain their competitive position in international markets (Ohmae 1989). Strategic alliances have grown in importance as a means of doing business across national boundaries receiving much attention both in the media and in academic circles (e.g., Hergert and Morris 1988; Harrigan 1988; Buckley and Casson 1988; Perlmutter and Heenan 1986; Borys and Jemison 1989; Bucklin and Sengupta 1993; Hamel 1991; Tsang 1999; Das and Teng 1999; Garai 1999; Inkpen 1998).

In spite of the increase in international strategic alliance activity in recent years it has been estimated that between 30% and 70% of alliances fail (Bleeke and Ernst 1991; Harrigan 1988; Killing 1988; Kogut 1988; Inkpen and Li 1999). This high failure rate suggests that insufficient empirical work has been undertaken to understand what characterizes successful and less successful international strategic alliances. This study aims to fill that gap by looking at the behavioral characteristics of international strategic alliances and assessing their impact on alliance success in order that managers can, in the future, develop more effective international partnerships.

Although in recent years the amount of research into international strategic alliances has increased, most studies have tended to focus on motives behind alliance formation, partner selection and the characteristics of the resulting co-operation (Contractor and Lorange 1988; Hennart 1988; Bleeke and Ernst 1991; Kogut 1988; Harrigan 1988; Blodgett 1991, Parkhe 1993; Glaister and Buckley 1996; Spekman et al. 1998, McCutcheon and Swamidas 1998). Studies focusing on success are, however, still limited (Anderson 1990; Parkhe 1993; Inkpen and Li

1999). What studies have been undertaken have focussed on the control-performance relationship with less attention being paid to behavioral aspects of the relationship (Killing 1983; Kogut 1988; Beamish 1985). Furthermore, recent empirical studies have tended to be based within the context of China and the US (e.g., Lin and Germain 1998; Chen and Boggs 1998; Glaister and Wu 1994; Lyles et al. 1999). Even where there is research of a more behavioral nature the studies have tended to concentrate on the problems associated with managing a strategic alliance rather than on what makes an alliance successful (Johnson 1999).

While some studies have started to consider behavioral characteristics these have tended to focus on co-marketing and supplier-dealer type relationships (Mohr and Spekman 1994; Lane and Beamish 1990; Bucklin and Sengupta 1993) or on strategic alliances within one country (Olson and Singsuwan 1997). There appear to be no studies which specifically consider behavioral characteristics in international strategic alliances. This study seeks to address this gap by studying the behavioral characteristics of international strategic alliances between UK firms and their US, European and Japanese partners and what impact they have on success. The specific aim of the research, therefore, is to assess the influence of behavioral characteristics on the success of UK international strategic alliances.

DEFINING INTERNATIONAL STRATEGIC ALLIANCES

There is some confusion as to exactly what constitutes an international strategic alliance (Williams et al. 1998; Vyas et al. 1995). They have been described in the literature as international co-operative or collaborative agreements or ventures (Root 1988; Hergert and Morris 1988; Buckley and Casson 1988; Harrigan 1988), hybrid arrangements (Borys and Jemison 1989), strategic alliances (Ohmae 1989; Yoshino and Rangan 1995; Pucik 1988; Terpstra and Simonin, 1993), joint ventures (Harrigan 1988; Hennart 1988, Kogut 1988) and coalitions or partnerships (Porter and Fuller, 1986; Perlmutter and Heenan 1986). In spite of the lack of standardization in terminology the basic assumption is that co-operation between partners improves performance.

For the purposes of the present study the term strategic alliance will be used to describe both equity and non-equity agreements in order to aid identification of the different types of international strategic alliances formed by UK firms the classification adopted by Terpstra and

Simonin (1993) will be used: (i) contractual agreements between two parties for which no legal entity is created and there is no purchase of equity between parties, (ii) equity participation which involves the acquisition of equity in one firm by another, (iii) joint ventures in which a separate legal entity is created and (iv) consortia, a collaborative arrangement among three or more parties, regardless of the equity structure.

BEHAVIOURAL CHARACTERISTICS OF INTERNATIONAL STRATEGIC ALLIANCES

Partnership Attributes

The notion of close relationships between individual members of a partnership has been explored by a number of researchers (Kanter 1988; Yoshino and Rangan 1995, Faulkner and Mcgee 1995). Within the strategic alliance literature partnership attributes have been considered within four broad areas: co-ordination, interdependence, commitment and trust (Parkhe 1993; Mohr and Spekman 1994; Monckza et al. 1998; Olson and Singsuwan 1997; Dyzma 1988; Anderson and Narus 1990; Johnson 1999).

Co-ordination within the strategic alliance literature has been described as the extent to which two firms are integrated within a relationship (Salmond and Spekman 1986). Resource dependency theory suggests that, in order to reduce uncertainty and manage dependency, firms need to co-ordinate their activities. Greater co-ordination can be achieved by balancing the level of autonomy of each partner within the relationship (Pfeffer and Salancik 1978). There has, however, been little empirical investigation into how co-ordination may impact on the success of an international strategic alliance. In their study of dealers and suppliers, however, Mohr and Spekman (1994) found co-ordination to be a good predictor of success. Monckza et al. (1998) and Olson and Singsuwan (1997) also observed the importance of co-ordination in their studies, but tended to only use single measures of co-ordination. This suggests the first proposition to be tested in this research:

P1. The level of co-ordination between partners will be higher in successful international strategic alliances than in less successful partnerships.

The co-ordination of activities between the alliance partners also leads to *interdependence* (Salmond and Spekman 1986). Within the literature interdependency is defined as the degree of replaceability and dependency of each firm on its partner both in terms of investment and resources (Kumar et al. 1995; Geyskens et al. 1996). Empirical evidence from the strategic alliance and dealer-supplier literature provide strong evidence that interdependence enhances the performance of alliances (Monckza et al. 1998; Olson and Singsuwan, 1997) and can facilitate value creation (Holm et al. 1999). Although none of this research is related directly to international strategic alliances the wider literature suggests the following proposition:

P2. The level of interdependence between partners will be greater in successful international strategic alliances than in less successful partnerships.

The construct of *commitment* has received much attention in the organizational behavior literature as well as in the marketing channel literature (e.g., Mowday et al. 1982; Anderson and Narus 1990; Kumar et al. 1995; Noordeweir et al. 1990). Here commitment is generally defined as an implicit pledge of relational continuity between exchange partners (Dwyer et al. 1987), with firms showing their commitment through their willingness to adopt a long term perspective to a relationship (Morgan and Hunt, 1994). Commitment to a relationship has been viewed in terms of the economic costs of maintaining the partnership as well as the emotional ties to the relationship (Morgan and Hunt 1994; Anderson and Weitz 1992). This is known as affective commitment and will be the focus of commitment in this study. Several researchers have observed a strong correlation between commitment and performance in buyer-supplier alliances (Dwyer et al. 1987; Morgan and Hunt, 1994; Monckza et al. 1998). This suggests the third proposition to be tested in this study:

P3. The level of commitment between partners will be higher in successful international strategic alliances than in less successful partnerships.

Trust as a concept has been found to be critical in understanding interpersonal and inter-organizational relationships (Mayer et al. 1995; Das and Teng 1998). Within the strategic alliance literature transaction cost theory suggests that the presence of trust is a critical factor in the relational governance of the partnership because of problems of co-ordination and mutual dependency (Anderson and Weitz 1990; Morgan and Hunt 1994; Monckza et al. 1998). This is because trust has the ability to reduce transaction costs by deterring opportunistic behavior, thus making partners take a long term perspective to the relationship (Beamish and Banks 1987). Trust has been dealt with in studies involving dealer-supplier partnerships and within strategic alliances in one country and the empirical evidence which exists suggests that trust is a key predictor of success. Hence the following proposition:

P4. The level of trust between partners will be greater in successful International Strategic Alliances than in less successful partnerships.

Communication Attributes

Communication is a central process in organizational activities and is critical to the success of organizations (Mohr and Nevin 1990). Ineffective communication can reduce the effectiveness of strategic alliances and thus lead to conflict between partners (Jain 1987). This suggests that an awareness of communication processes is essential within partnerships if maximum efforts are to be co-ordinated and directed towards the success of international strategic alliances.

Several researchers have noted that the meaningful and timely exchange of information can result in a more trusting relationship between partners helping managers to realize mutual benefits by reducing misunderstandings (Mohr and Spekman 1994; Anderson and Narus 1991; Dwyer et al. 1987). The quality of the information shared has also been found to be a key issue within the context of buyer-supplier partnerships and national strategic alliances (Mohr and Spekman 1994; Olson and Singsuwan 1997; Monckza et al. 1998), and has been found to be an important predictor of partnership success (Devlin and Bleakley 1988). A high level of information sharing has also been found to be positively correlated to satisfaction within a partnership (Monckza et al. 1998). This suggests the proposition to be tested in this study:

P5. Sharing of information and the quality of information shared will be higher in successful international strategic alliances than in less successful partnerships.

Participation refers to the extent to which partners actively engage in planning and goal setting. Participation in planning and goal setting have been found to be key predictors of success in dealer-supplier relationships (Mohr and Spekman 1994; Monckza et al. 1998) and this study will now test to see of the same holds true for international strategic alliances:

P6. Participation in planning and goal setting will be greater in successful international strategic alliances than in less successful partnerships

Conflict

Conflict has been identified as a key issue within the strategic alliance literature and arises when firms engaged in a partnership try to maintain their autonomy. Conflict can occur for a number of reasons including cultural differences, management style and differences in operational procedures (Jain 1987). Conflict has been specifically identified as a key reason for the failure of a number of strategic alliances as it can result in misunderstandings and distrust which, in turn, lead to reduced co-operation and poor performance (Killing 1983; Anderson and Narus 1990). Several studies of partnerships including some international strategic alliances have identified that there is a negative relationship between conflict and alliance performance (Ding 1997; Tilman 1990). Conflict has also been found to be a major catalyst for the termination of international joint ventures (Lane and Beamish 1990; Reynolds 1984). Both Mohr and Spekman (1994) and Monckza et al. (1998) found that successful partnerships were more likely to recognize the potential for conflict and use problem solving techniques to try to avoid conflict arising. Hence the final proposition of this study:

P7. Conflict will be lower in successful international strategic alliances than in less successful partnerships.

MEASURING INTERNATIONAL STRATEGIC ALLIANCE SUCCESS

The definition and operationalization of performance is an important issue in the international strategic alliances literature (Anderson 1990;

Geringer and Herbert 1989; 1991). There is, however, little consensus within the literature on what performance is and how it should be measured. Measures of success have been classified into three broad categories: (i) financial measures, (ii) objective measures and (iii) subjective measures.

Financial measures reflect the fulfillment of the economic goals of the international strategic alliance and can be measured using a range of financial indicators including profitability, return on investment (ROI) and cost position (Good 1972; Dang 1977; Renforth 1974). Financial measures, however, have their limitations such that many researchers have focused their attention on other objective measures such as the survival, duration and stability of the international strategic alliance (Franko 1971; Killing 1983; Blodgett 1991; Kogut 1988; Geringer and Hebert 1991; Harrigan 1988; Gomes-Casseres 1987).

Both financial and objective measures of performance have their shortcomings when considering international strategic alliances. Financial indicators do not reflect the extent to which an international strategic alliance has met its short-term objectives which may be more strategic than financial in nature (Killing 1983; Blodgett 1991; Contractor and Lorange 1988). Anderson (1990) argues that financial measures only evaluate one dimension of performance and that other measures, including qualitative ones, should also be examined in the case of international strategic alliances. This is because, in spite of poor financial performance, the partnership may have achieved its objectives. Furthermore, Geringer and Hebert (1991) argue that an international strategic alliance may be deemed by managers to not be successful in spite of a good financial performance. In addition, obtaining accurate financial details on alliances is very difficult since many firms are reluctant to provide this information leaving researchers questioning the quality and accuracy of any performance figures obtained (Anderson 1990). There is also much criticism of objective measures as in order to properly assess the performance of an individual international strategic alliance some observers note that the partnership must either have been terminated or failed. Because firms enter into international strategic alliances for a variety of reasons duration and survival do not effectively assess performance (Park and Gerado 1997; Gomes-Casseres 1987; Harrigan 1988). As Reuer (1998) observes, "if exit barriers are high, successful strategic alliances are not necessarily indicated by long-lived ventures, and short-lived ventures can be judged as successes from both sponsors' perspectives if they have achieved their strategic purpose" (p. 207).

In view of the difficulties associated with financial and objective measures of international strategic alliance performance several researchers have advocated the use of subjective measures of performance (Killing 1983; Schaan 1983; Geringer and Hebert 1991; Bucklin and Sengupta 1993; Cullen et al. 1994; Lee and Beamish 1995; Mjoen and Tallman 1997; Saxton 1997). The most commonly used subjective measure is an overall assessment of the firm's satisfaction with the performance of the international strategic alliance. This has the advantage of assessing the extent to which the alliance's objectives have been met (Killing 1983; Schaan 1993; Geringer and Hebert 1991). One possible limitation of subjective measures is that respondents may be biased in their assessment of their firm's performance. However, a study by Geringer and Hebert (1991) has found that perceptual assessments of performance and satisfaction correlate well with objective measures.

In this study subjective measures have been used to evaluate the success of international strategic alliances. This is largely because, from initial contacts made with the UK firms, it was clear that financial information would be almost impossible to obtain. Performance was, therefore, measured in a number of ways. Firstly respondents were asked to indicate what criteria they used to assess their own performance. They were then required to rate, on a five-point scale (1 = not very successful; 5 = very successful), according to those criteria, how successful they perceived their international strategic alliance to be. In addition, based on an extensive review of the literature, respondents were asked to evaluate, on a five point scale (1 = very dissatisfied; 5 = very satisfied), how satisfied they were with eight key aspects of the alliance (Killing 1983; Schaan 1983; Geringer and Hebert 1991; Beamish 1985). Managers were also requested to provide an overall rating of their satisfaction with the relationship. As a final measure of success respondents were asked to assess, on a five-point scale (1 = not at all; 5 = very well), the extent to which they thought the alliance had met their firm's overall objectives with regard to profitability, market share and sales growth.

METHODOLOGY

The first stage of the research was to develop a database of all international strategic alliance activity from 1988 to 1995 between UK firms and their US, European and Japanese partners. The database was developed using information gathered from *The Economist* and *Financial*

Times along the lines of similar databases constructed by other researchers (e.g., Hergert and Morris 1988; Glaister and Buckley 1994). A total of 778 alliances were identified (Kauser and Shaw 2000). Within Europe over 60% of the international strategic alliances were formed with firms in Germany, France and Italy so the sample frame was limited to these countries. This reduced the total population to 613 alliances. Contact details were obtained for 556 of these alliances and all were contacted by telephone to request their participation in the study. One hundred and six alliances declined to participate in the study, at this stage, citing confidentiality as the reason for their lack of participation. Questionnaires were sent out to the remaining 450 alliances requesting information on performance, behavioral characteristics including co-ordination, interdependence, commitment, trust, communication and conflict.

A total of 287 responses (63.7%) were received. In spite of having agreed to participate in the study when contacted by telephone 173 respondents did not complete the questionnaire giving the following reasons for non-response: the alliance had been terminated, contract confidentiality did not allow such detailed information to be divulged, workload, and some commented that the alliance was not strategic in nature. The length of the questionnaire may have been an issue for some firms but the usable response rate of 114 completed questionnaires (25.3%) compares well to other studies of a similar nature (Mohr and Spekman 1994).

Respondent Profile

As Table 1 shows the majority of alliances in this sample were between UK firms and their US partners with just over a third of alliances being with European partners. The remaining alliances were consortia formed between three or more firms from more than one country. This geographic breakdown compares well with the population of alliances with these countries so can be considered to show a high degree of representativeness. The majority of alliances were formed within the financial services sector followed by construction and property and business and information services which again is representative of the population as a whole (see Kauser and Shaw 2000).

In terms of the form of international strategic alliance over a third were joint ventures with over 65% of all alliances in this sample involving some form of equity participation (see Table 2). This also compares well with the population in which 67.9% of equity partnerships were observed (Kauser and Shaw 2000). Nearly half of the alliances in this

TABLE 1. Nationalities of Foreign Partner Firms of Sample International Strategic Alliances

Foreign Country	Sample Number of Alliances	Percent	Population Number of Alliances	Percent
USA	184	40.8%	242	39.5%
Japan	88	19.6%	113	18.4%
France	82	18.2%	104	16.9%
Germany	52	11.6%	74	12.1%
Italy	33	7.3%	42	6.9%
Consortia	11	2.4%	38	6.2%
Total	450	100.0%	613	100.0%

TABLE 2. Type of International Strategic Alliance

Type of Alliance	Frequency	Percentage Total
50:50 Joint Venture	40	35.1%
Majority Equity	22	19.3%
Minority Equity	13	11.4%
Contractual Agreement	29	25.4%
Consortium	10	8.8%
Total	114	100.0%

sample were established for marketing purposes which again is a good reflection of the population of UK international strategic alliances.

Construct Measurement

Based on a thorough review of the literature, the domain of the various underlying behavioral measures was specified and a sample of items was generated for each construct thus ensuring high content validity for all measures (Churchill 1979). A questionnaire was developed and pretested on a number of senior managers with extensive alliance management experience. All measures were evaluated for reliability and validity using conventional psychometric evaluations. The reliabilities of all multiple-item scales were assessed using Cronbach's alpha and factor analysis (Nunnally 1978). The results of these analysis are presented in Table 3. All measures demonstrated a high degree of internal consistency, with alphas ranging from 0.70 to 0.93.

TABLE 3. Reliability Scales for Behavioral Constructs

Behavioral Constructs	Original Number of Scale Items	Number of Scale Items after Deletion	Cronbach's Alpha
Co-ordination	8	7	.88
Interdependence	10	9	.70
Commitment/Goals and Values 1	10	10	.93
Commitment/Goals and Values 2	5	5	.91
Commitment/Obligations	7	7	.91
Commitment/stay in relationship	6	6	.86
Trust 1	5	4	.90
Trust 2	8	7	.90
Conflict Resolution	6	N/A	N/A
Conflict	6	4	.70
Information Quality	5	5	.89
Information Sharing	4	3	.72
Participation	5	5	.79
Total	85	72	

As a further test of reliability and validity, exploratory factor analysis was conducted for each proposition on items relating to co-ordination, interdependence, commitment, trust, communication and conflict in order to examine the presence of underlying behavioral dimensions and confirm that questionnaire items used in the study measured the proposed constructs. The results of the factor analysis using varimax rotation and the percentage of the total variance attributable to the different number of factors are summarised for each model in Table 4. The appropriateness of the factor models was evaluated, using the Bartlett's test of sphericity and the Kaiser-Meyer-Olkin (KMO) measure of sampling adequacy (see Table 4). Both of these tests clearly indicate that factor analysis is an appropriate tool for this data (Hair et al. 1998).

Table 4 shows the factors resulting from the six factor analysis. In the first model (coordination) the variables loaded on one factor. This factor is associated with coordination between partner firms and reflects the mutual integration of the partners in the alliance agreement. This factor is labeled " coordination between partner firms." The second factor model (interdependence) resulted in three factors. These factors are concerned with the UK firm's degree of dependency on the partner firm's marketing capabilities, administrative and financial resources.

The third model (commitment) resulted in three factors. The first factor relates to the UK firm's commitment to their international partners in terms of their identification and involvement in the alliance relationship and is labeled "commitment to alliance goals." The second factor is "commitment to alliance by obligation" and relates to the UK firm's willingness to exert effort on behalf of the alliance. Factor three captures the UK firm's motivation to maintain their relationship with their partner and is thus called "commitment to stay in the relationship." In the fourth model (trust) all variables loaded on one factor concerned with the UK firm's belief in their partner's trustworthiness and is thus labeled "trust in partner." The fifth model (conflict) resulted in one factor named "conflict." Model six (communication) resulted in three factors. Factor one is "information quality" focusing on the accuracy, timeliness, adequacy, completeness and credibility of information that may be exchanged between the partner firms. The second factor relates

TABLE 4. Underlying Dimensions of Behavioral Factors of International Strategic Alliance Success

1. Coordination (Factor Model 1)

Variables	Factor 1
Teamwork with partner	.830
Exchange of ideas with partner	.818
UK firm integrated with partner	.809
High level of interaction between partners	.808
Partner firm integrated with UK firm	.807
Keep partner informed about important decisions	.727
Partner activities an extension of UK firm	.570
Eigenvalue	4.169
Percent of variance explained	59.6
KMO	.803
Bartlett's Test of Sphericity	472.402

2. Interdependence (Factor Model 2)

Variables	Factor 1	Factor 2	Factor 3
Dependency on marketing capability	.848		
Dependency on market information	.800		
Dependency on customer service	.759		
Dependency on sales/profits	.737		
Dependency on administrative support		.834	
Dependency on manpower resources		.823	
Dependency on financial resources			.836
Dependency on management skills			.598
Eigenvalue		2.558	
Percent of variance explained		31.9	
KMO		.654	
Bartlett's Test of Sphericity		246.705	

TABLE 4 (continued)

3. Commitment (Factor Model 3)

Variables	Factor 1	Factor 2	Factor 3
Agreement over key decisions	.825		
Agreement over goals/objectives	.773		
Agreement over future plans	.740		
Agreement over strategic direction	.731		
Agreement over roles performed	.717		
Share understanding and vision	.705		
Agreement over contractual terms	.692		
Agreement over daily operations	.590		
Identify with goals/objectives	.582		
Obligated to compromise in achieving objectives		.767	
Obligated to be patient with partner over mistakes		.759	
Obligated to listen to problems of partner		.741	
Obligated to try to overcome problems		.739	
Obligated to encourage goal achievement		.697	
Obligated to satisfy partners needs		.643	
Obligated to help build the relationship		.630	
Relationship important to achieve strategic objectives			.849
Long-term relationship will be profitable			.771
Staying in relationship a desire			.751
Staying in relationship is a necessity			.741
Partnership is valuable			.726
Make sacrifices to achieve long-term objectives			.506
Eigenvalue	11.069		
Percent of variance explained	50.3		
KMO	.992		
Bartlett's Test of Sphericity	1912.365		

4. Trust (Factor Model 4)

Variables	Factor 1
Partner trusted to show loyalty	.897
We can always rely on each other	.888
Partner makes effort to keep commitments	.881
Relationship marked by a high degree of harmony	.834
Partner trusted to be supportive	.806
Partner trusted to keep promises	.802
Partner trusted to be sincere	.786
Relationship open and informal	.727
We do not take advantage of each other	.727
We share work related problems	.719
Close personal ties between us	.623
Eigenvalue	6.937
Percent of variance explained	63.1
KMO	.923
Bartlett's Test of Sphericity	952.158

5. Conflict (Factor Model 5)

Variables	Factor 1
Distrust	.797
Personality conflicts	.786
Cultural misunderstandings	.699
Conflicting goals	.692
Eigenvalue Percent of variance explained KMO Bartlett's Test of Sphericity	2.221 55.5 .720 93.706

6. Communication (Factor Model 6)

Variables	Factor 1	Factor 2	Factor 3
Communication adequate/inadequate	.875		
Communication complete/incomplete	.868		
Communication credible/incredible	.779		
Communication accurate/inaccurate	.760		
Communication timely/untimely	.682		
Seek partners advice in decision-making		.804	
Partner seeks advice before decision-making		.705	
Both keep each informed about changes		.690	
Inform partner of changing needs		.657	
Participate in goal setting		.574	
Participate in planning activities			.773
Share proprietary information			.690
Participate in regular meetings			.538
Eigenvalue Percent of variance explained KMO Bartlett's Test of Sphericity	5.541 42.6 .831 781.429		

to the partners' ability to engage in decision-making and goal and is labeled "participation." Factor three concerns the way in which the UK firms communicate information with their partner firms and is labeled "information sharing."

FINDINGS

Respondents were asked to indicate how *they* measured the performance of their international strategic alliance. As Table 5 shows all of the 114 UK partners used the traditional measures of profitability, market share and sales growth to assess their performance. Over 60% of the respondents also claimed to use other measures such as access to markets, an assessment of their competitive position and ROI. Given that all

TABLE 5. Criteria Used for Assessing International Strategic Alliance Performance

Performance Criteria	**% of alliances using the criteria**	**% rating their alliance as successful**
Profitability	100	57.0
Market Share	100	57.0
Growth	100	56.1
Access to market	70.2	61.3
Competitive Position	64.9	43.2
ROI	63.2	37.5
Marketing	52.6	45.0
Cost control	42.1	39.6
Technology development	37.7	60.5
Product design and development	36.8	54.8
Access to distribution channels	30.7	54.7

Success measured on a five-point scale: 1 = very unsuccessful; 5 = very successful

of the sample strategic alliances used profitability, market share and sales growth these three measures were used for further analysis.

Testing the Propositions

The factor scores generated from the six exploratory factor analyses were fed into a regression analysis. Each of the propositions was then tested in order to establish the extent to which behavioral characteristics accurately predict international strategic alliance success. The predictors and independent measures are presented in Table 6.

For each proposition, fourteen separate regression models (one for each outcome success item) were examined. For each regression model, the behavioral factors produced by the factor analyses were included as potential predictors. The results in Table 7 depict the significant predictors with the resulting beta weights, and the percentage of variance explained for each of the success items. The overall goodness of fit for each of the success measures was quite high, ranging from 53.2% to 72.9%. This indicates that a high proportion of the variation in each of the dependent measures is explained by the explanatory variables (Hair et al. 1998). Furthermore, the F statistic for each of the regression equations exceeded the F critical with 93 degrees of freedom at the 0.01 level and therefore it can be concluded that each regression model has signifi-

TABLE 6. The Independent and Dependent Measures Used In Regression Analysis

Independent Variables	Dependent Measures
Behavioral Factors	**Alliance Performance**
Coordination	Market share **Y1**
Factor 1 = Coordination between partner firms = **þ1**	Profitability **Y2**
Interdependence	Sales growth **Y3**
Factor 1 = Dependency on marketing capabilities = **þ2**	
Factor 2 = Dependency on administrative support = **þ3**	
Factor 3 = Dependency on financial resources = **þ4**	**Alliance Satisfaction**
Commitment	• Satisfaction with Relationship
Factor 1 = Commitment to alliance goals = **þ5**	Co-ordination of activities **Y4**
Factor 2 = Commitment to alliance by obligation = **þ6**	Interaction between managers **Y5**
Factor 3 = Commitment to stay in relationship = **þ7**	Compatibility of activities **Y6**
Trust	Participation in decision making **Y7**
Factor 1 = Trust in partner = **þ8**	Levels of commitment **Y8**
Communication	Sharing of information **Y9**
Factor 1 = Information quality = **þ9**	Managing alliance activities **Y10**
Factor 12 = Participation = **þ10**	Level of honesty **Y11**
Factor 13 = Information sharing = **þ11**	• Satisfaction with Overall Objectives
Conflict	Market share **Y12**
Factor 1 = Conflict = **þ12**	Profitability **Y13**
	Sales growth **Y14**

cant explanatory power (Hair et al. 1998). Univariate tests confirmed the findings found within the regression techniques.

Co-Ordination

The regression analysis provides support for proposition P1 that a higher level of co-ordination is associated with more successful international strategic alliances. Co-ordination (factor þ1) was positively related to measures of both strategic alliance performance and satisfaction (see Table 7). These findings are consistent with those of Mohr and Spekman (1994) who found co-ordination as a significant predictor for partnership success. However, Mohr and Spekman (1994) showed only a low level of reliability in their measure of co-ordination. This study has shown co-ordination to be a good predictor of international strategic alliance performance in terms of profitability, market share and sales growth as well as satisfaction with the relationship. These findings provide greater empirical support for the importance of co-ordination in predicting the success of international strategic alliances. Thus managers

TABLE 7. Regression Coefficients for Behavioural Factors

Dependent Measures	Y1	Y2	Y3	Y4	Y5	Y6	Y7	Y8	Y9	Y10	Y11	Y12	Y13	Y14
Constant	3.447	3.430	3.482	3.316	3.518	3.430	3.254	3.518	3.149	3.360	3.702	3.395	3.395	3.342
Þ1	.639*** (.089)	.617*** (.094)	.467*** (.083)	.535*** (.072)	.665*** (.070)	.564*** (.085)	.574*** (.077)	.615*** (.090)	.658*** (.079)	.616*** (.073)	.570*** (.089)	.617*** (.091)	.661*** (.102)	.614*** (.088)
Adjusted R^2	.310	.269	.212	.322	.439	.275	.328	.289	.375	.384	.263	.286	.266	.299
F Statistic	.000	.000	.000	.000	.000	.000	.000	.000	.000	.000	.000	.000	.000	.000
Dependent Measures	Y1	Y2	Y3	Y4	Y5	Y6	Y7	Y8	Y9	Y10	Y11	Y12	Y13	Y14
Constant	3.447	3.430	3.482	3.316	3.518	3.430	3.254	3.518	3.149	3.360	3.702	3.395	3.395	3.342
Þ2	.161 (.106)	.132 (.110)	.195* (.093)	.028 (.088)	.051 (.095)	.031 (.101)	–.114 (.092)	–.210 (.105)	.087 (.101)	.158 (.093	.088 (.102)	.120 (.107)	.089 (.120)	.150 (.104)
Þ3	–.163 (.106)	–.166 (.110)	.095 (.093)	.225 (.088)	.055 (.095)	.029 (.101)	.090 (.092)	.076 (.105)	.069 (.101)	.016) (.093)	.190 (.102)	–.146 (.107)	.152 (.120)	–.108 (.104)
Þ4	0.46 (.106)	.056 (.110)	.028 (.093)	.151 (.088)	.012 (.095)	.625 (.101)	.208* (.092)	.151 (.105)	.093 (.101)	.052 (.093)	.088 (.102)	.036 (.107)	.012 (.120)	.500 (.104)
Adjusted R^2	.016	.008	.021	.010	.021	.024	.040	.027)	.013	.002	.017	.002	.007	.003
F Statistic	.000	.000	.000	.000	.000	.000	.000	.000	.000	.000	.000	.000	.000	.000
Dependent Measures	Y1	Y2	Y3	Y4	Y5	Y6	Y7	Y8	Y9	Y10	Y11	Y12	Y13	Y14
Constant	3.447	3.430	3.42	3.316	3.518	3.430	3.254	3.518	3.149	3.360	3.702	3.395	3.395	3.342
Þ5	.482*** (.089)	394*** (.094)	.188* (.085)	.525*** (.065)	.538*** (.072)	.567*** (.072)	.586*** (.073)	.601*** (.088)	.627*** (.076)	.565*** (.068)	.629*** (.083)	.492*** (.087)	.434*** (.097)	.406*** (.086)
Þ6	.225* (.089)	.289** (.094)	.224** (.085)	.218** (.065)	.304*** (.072)	.169* (.072)	.113 (.073)	.055 (.088)	.227** (.076)	.264*** (.068)	.089 (.083)	.237** (.087)	.226* (.097)	.245** (.086)
Þ7	.366*** (.089)	.416*** (.094)	.334*** (.085)	.294*** (.065)	.213* (.072)	.461*** (.072)	.207** (.073)	.262** (.088)	.247*** (.076)	.280*** (.068)	.217** (.083)	.413*** (.087)	.577*** (.097)	.435*** (.086)
Adjusted R^2	.304	.279	.176	.455	.414	.483	.388	.320	.430	.465	.358	.343	.339	.317
F Statistic	.000	.000	.000	.000	.000	.000	.000	.000	.000	.000	.000	.000	.000	.000

Dependent Measures	Y1	Y2	Y3	Y4	Y5	Y6	Y7	Y8	Y9	Y10	Y11	Y12	Y13	Y14
Constant	3.447	3.430	3.482	3.316	3.518	3.430	3.254	3.518	3.149	3.360	3.702	3.395	3.395	3.342
Þ8	**.601*** (.091)**	**.552*** (.098)**	**.369*** (.088)**	**.673*** (.061)**	**.666*** (.070)**	**.648*** (.080)**	**.700*** (.067)**	**.793*** (.076)**	**.831*** (.063)**	**.684*** (.067)**	**.878*** (.062)**	**.599*** (.092)**	**.616*** (.105)**	**.598*** (.089)**
Adjusted R^2	.273	.214	.129	.514	.441	.365	.492	.487	.603	.474	.638	.269	.230	.283
F Statistic	.000	.000	.000	.000	.000	.000	.000	.000	.000	.000	.000	.000	.000	.000

Dependent Measures	Y1	Y2	Y3	Y4	Y5	Y6	Y7	Y8	Y9	Y10	Y11	Y12	Y13	Y14
Constant	3.447	3.430	3.482	3.316	3.518	3.430	3.254	3.518	3.149	3.360	3.702	3.395	3.395	3.342
Þ9	**.218** (.086)**	**.278** (.095)**	**.108 (.086)**	**.212** (.072)**	**.261*** (.071)**	**.252** (.082)**	**.308*** (.070)**	**.371*** (.087)**	**.338*** (.075)**	**.117 (.073)**	**.325*** (.083)**	**.297*** (.088)**	**.384*** (.104)**	**.226** (.089)**
Þ10	**.382*** (.086)**	**.299** (.095)**	**.300*** (.086)**	**.311*** (.072)**	**.487*** (.071)**	**.384*** (.082)**	**.503*** (.070)**	**.515*** (.087)**	**.532*** (.075)**	**.375*** (.073)**	**.548*** (.083)**	**.458*** (.088)**	**.359*** (.104)**	**.490*** (.089)**
Þ11	**.529*** (.086)**	**.473*** (.095)**	**.292*** (.086)**	**.397*** (.072)**	**.362*** (.071)**	**.424*** (.082)**	**.321*** (.070)**	**.206* (.087)**	**.354*** (.075)**	**.480*** (.073)**	**.195* (.083)**	**.386*** (.088)**	**.366*** (.104)**	**.288** (.089)**
Adjusted R^2	.349	.264	.166	.325	.423	.327	.441	.330	.445	.377	.352	.325	.236	.283
F Statistic	.000	.000	.000	.000	.000	.000	.000	.000	.000	.000	.000	.000	.000	.000

Dependent Measures	Y1	Y2	Y3	Y4	Y5	Y6	Y7	Y8	Y9	Y10	Y11	Y12	Y13	Y14
Constant	3.447	3.430	3.482	3.316	3.518	3.430	3.254	3.518	3.149	3.360	3.702	3.395	3.395	3.342
Þ12	**−.254* (.105)**	**−.299** (.107)**	−.138 (.093)	**−.309*** (.083)**	**−.352*** (.088)**	**−.394*** (.093)**	**−.391*** (.086)**	**−.432*** (.099)**	**−.492*** (.089)**	**−.315*** (.088)**	**−.555*** (.089)**	**−.311** (.104)**	**−.393*** (.114)**	**−.252** (.102)**
Adjusted R^2	.041	.056	.010	.101	.117	.130	.147	.139	.206	.094	.249	.066	.088	.043
F Statistic	.000	.000	.000	.000	.000	.000	.000	.000	.000	.000	.000	.000	.000	.000

*** Significant at 0.001 level
** Significant at 0.01 level
* Significant at 0.05 level

of all international strategic alliances need to understand the benefits of maintaining a high level of co-ordination between partner firms. For the managers of poorer performing international strategic alliances it is essential that they develop and adopt co-ordinating mechanisms which promote a co-ordinated set of goals and activities for their partnership.

Interdependence

The literature suggests a strong link between co-ordination and interdependence (Salmond and Spekman 1986). However, the results of this study provide little support for proposition P2 which states that successful international strategic alliances are more likely to be interdependent compared to less successful partnerships (see Table 7). The UK firms' dependence on their partner firms' marketing capabilities (factor þ2) was not related to the performance of the international strategic alliance and was even negatively related to some aspects of alliance satisfaction. The UK firms' dependency on their partners' administrative capabilities (factor þ3) was found to have a negative relationship with alliance performance in terms of profitability and market share. The beta coefficients in Table 7 indicate that the higher the interdependence the lower the level of perceived success. Dependency on financial resources (factor þ4), were also shown to have little influence on the performance of and satisfaction with the international strategic alliance. This suggests that management and financial resources are also less likely to be co-ordinated between international strategic alliance partners.

Commitment

Commitment (factors þ5, þ6 and þ7) was found to positively influence international strategic alliance performance and satisfaction. The significant regression coefficients indicate that commitment to alliance goals (factor þ5) and the desire to maintain the relationship (factor þ6) are more strongly associated with a good performance than commitment to the alliance by obligation (factor þ7). In terms of the different measures of performance used in this study commitment was most positively associated with profitability. These results are encouraging as it shows that success occurs because the partners manage their relationship through mutual consent rather than relying on coercion through written agreements. From this study it is, therefore, clear that for international strategic alliances to succeed, partners need to identify with the goals and objectives of the alliance and have positive feelings of identification and involvement with the relationship. Moreover, partners have to be willing to make an effort and invest in the relationship in order to achieve their goals and objectives. The implication of this for managers is that commitment to alliance goals and commitment to fulfil these goals through sustaining the relationship is pivotal to a high level of profitability performance in UK international strategic alliances. These findings support previous research (Mohr and Spekman 1994; Olson and Singsuwan 1997; Monckza et al. 1998) and provide strong support for Proposition P3. However, while Mohr and Spekman (1994) predicted that commitment is associated with partnership success, they examined only a fraction of the measures used in this study. They assessed commitment with 3-item scales, whereas in this study three factors of commitment consisted of 23 measures in total. This study, therefore, has developed a new, reliable set of constructs to measure commitment in a relationship.

Trust

The regression analysis (see Table 7) indicates that trust (factor þ8) is positively related to international strategic alliance performance and satisfaction and is thus a good predictor of alliance success. These findings support proposition P4 that a higher level of trust between partners engaged in UK international strategic alliances is likely to result in better alliance performance. Trust between partners is, therefore, an essential attribute if an international strategic alliance is to succeed. The findings support those of Mohr and Spekman (1994) who found that a trusting relationship for computer suppliers and dealers served to calm the dealer's fear of opportunistic behavior thus resulting in a successful partnership. The results suggest that in order to build trust in an international strategic alliance managers must try to instill in personnel involved in the relationship the importance of keeping promises, being sincere when making decisions, showing loyalty and offering support to the other party. Again, additional robust measures of relationship trust have been developed in this research.

Communication Attributes

The results provide support for Propositions 5 and 6 that sharing of information (factor þ11) and the quality of information transmitted (factor þ9) is greater in more successful international strategic alliances compared to less successful alliances (see Table 7). The above findings suggest that the quality of information transmitted and the extent of information shared can enable both partners to understand each others goals and objectives, allowing them to coordinate their efforts to achieve their mutual objectives in terms of performance and satisfaction with the alliance relationship. Participation between partner firms (factor þ10) also showed strong support for both alliance performance and satisfaction. While the findings of this study are consistent with those of Mohr and Spekman (1994) in that communication strategies are critical to partnership success, Mohr and Spekman (1994) showed communication quality to be associated only with satisfaction with manufacturer support and participation to be associated with sales volume. Sharing of information was negatively associated with satisfaction with profits and manufacturer support. The current study has provided greater empirical findings by providing stronger support for both alliance performance and satisfaction. Based on the above evidence, it can be concluded that the quality of information exchanged between partners, the sharing of information and the extent of participation in goals setting and planning activities can help in the achievement of the goals and objectives of the alliance and result in better outcomes for both parties, since more information, knowledge, skills and insights will be shared between partners.

Conflict

The regression analysis shows that conflict (factor þ12) negatively impacts on the performance and satisfaction of international strategic alliances. The beta coefficients in Table 7, show a negative, significant relationship between conflict and the measures of performance and satisfaction with the alliance relationship. This suggests that conflict in international strategic alliances can hinder alliance performance which, in turn, can impact on a manager's satisfaction with the relationship. The existence of conflict, thus appears to be sufficient to derail the financial and market performance of an international strategic alliance. The results fully support proposition P7 which observes that conflict will be lower in successful international alliances, and it is consistent with the findings that conflict is an inherent characteristic of all alliances (Habib 1983; Killing 1983). In light of these findings managers need to be aware of its potential existence and the need to minimize misunderstandings. However, in order to control the level of conflict in an international strategic alliance both partners need to understand the basis of where and why conflict arises.

CONCLUSIONS AND MANAGERIAL IMPLICATIONS

Previous research has shown the importance of behavioral characteristics in influencing the successful management of inter-organizational relationships. This study has built on that body of knowledge and represents the first systematic collection of data assessing the influence of behavioral characteristics on the performance of international strategic alliances. The results of this study have shown that partners in UK international strategic alliances that are well integrated with each other by co-ordinating their activities are more likely to have a higher level of performance and be more satisfied with their partnership. Partners in successful UK international strategic alliances are more likely to identify with and accept the goals and values of the partnership resulting in higher levels of commitment to achieving those goals and objectives. A trusting relationship that enjoys a high degree of harmony, loyalty and sincerity is also shown to have a positive impact on the performance of international strategic alliances. Furthermore, the study has demonstrated that communication in terms of the quality of information transmitted, the extent of information shared and participation of both parties in the planning of goals and activities is crucial for the success of an international strategic alliance. Conflict was found to have a major influence on the performance of international strategic alliances which suggests that conflict can hinder a good performance.

The most important action to be taken by taken by managers in building a successful international alliance is to foster and nurture the alliance relationship through the development of greater levels of co-ordination, commitment, trust, communication and through the avoidance of frequent conflicts. This study has suggested that the ability to co-ordinate activities, develop a sense of trust and commitment to the relationship, the extent of communication and the way in which it is conveyed are critical to the relationship and can help promote the effective management of international strategic alliances.

This research has provided an important extension to current theoretical perspectives on behavioral factors in inter-organisational relationships. It has provided researchers with new insights into the way coordination, interdependence, commitment, trust, communication processes and conflict contribute to international strategic alliance performance. These findings complement existing research and provide a greater contribution to the understanding of the phenomenon of success in international strategic alliances. They have also shown that how managers measure the successful of their international partnerships can impact on their perception of the performance of the relationship. A full discussion of the different performance measures used in the course of this study is outside the scope of this paper, but should be the subject of future research.

This paper has focused on the impact of behavioral characteristics on international strategic alliance success. Further research is needed to understand the importance of these attributes compared to structural and control characteristics. The study has also only considered, at this stage, the perceptions of the managers within the UK partner firms. In order to obtain a complete picture of alliance performance managers in the partner firms in the overseas markets also need to be approached. Additional research is needed to assess whether the importance of behavioral characteristics is unique to British alliance partners or whether they assume equal importance in alliances with partners from other countries.

REFERENCES

Anderson, E. (1990). One frontier: On assessing joint venture performance. *Sloan Management Review*.31(2) 19-30.

Anderson, J.C. & Narus, J.A. (1990). A model of distributor firm and manufacturer firm working partnerships. *Journal of Marketing, 54, 42-58.*

Anderson, E. & Weitz, B.A. (1992). The use of pledges to build and sustain commitment in distribution channels. *Journal of Marketing Research*, XXIX, 18-34.

Bartlett, C. & Ghoshal, S. (1987). Managing across borders: New strategic requirements, *Sloan Management Review*, 29 (1), 7-17.

Beamish, P.W. (1985). The characteristics of joint ventures in developed and developing countries. *Columbia Journal of World Business*, 13-19.

Beamish, P.W. & Banks, J.C. (1987). Equity joint ventures and the theory of the multinational enterprise, *Journal of International Business Studies*, Summer, 1-16.

Bleeke, J. & Ernst, D. (1991). The way to win in cross border alliances, *Harvard Business Review*, Nov-Dec, 127-135.

Blodgett, L.L. (1991). Towards a resource-based theory of bargaining power in international joint ventures, *Journal of Global Marketing*, 5, 35-54.

Borys, B. & Jemison, D. (1989). Hybrid arrangements as strategic alliances: Theoretical issues in organizational combinations, *Academy of Management Review*, 14, 234-249.

Buckley, P.J. & Casson, M. (1988) A theory of co-operation in international business, In F.J. Contractor & P. Lorange (Ed.) *Co-operative Strategies in International Business* (31-53). Lexington Books.

Bucklin, L.P. & Sengupta, S. (1993). Organizing successful co-marketing alliances, *Journal of Marketing*, 57, 32-46.

Chen, R. and Boggs, D. J. (1998) Long term cooperation prospects in international joint ventures: Perspectives of Chinese firms, *Journal of Applied Management Studies*, 7, 1, 111-126.

Churchill, G.A. (1979). A paradigm for developing better measures of marketing constructs. *Journal of Marketing Research, 16, 64-73*

Contractor, F.J. & Lorange, P. (1988). Why should firms co-operate? In F.J. Contractor & P. Lorange (Ed.) *Co-operative Strategies in International Business* (3-20). Lexington Books.

Cullen, J.B. Johnson, J.L. & Sakano, T. (1994). Japanese and local partner commitment to IJVs: Psychological consequences of outcomes and investments in the IJV relationships. *Journal of International Business Studies*, 91-115.

Dang, T. (1977). Ownership, control and performance of the multinational Corporation: A study of US wholly-owned subsidiaries and joint ventures in the Philippines and Taiwan, *Unpublished Doctoral Dissertation, University of California, Los Angeles.*

Das, T. and Teng, B. (1998) Between trust and control: Developing confidence in alliances, *Academy of Management Review*, 23, 3, 491-512

Das, T. and Teng, B (1999) Managing risks in strategic alliances, *Academy of Management Executive*, 13, 4, 50-62

Devlin, G. & Bleackley (1988). Strategic alliances-Guidelines for success, *Long Range Planning*, 21 (5), 18-23.

Ding, D.Z. (1997). Control, conflict and performance: A study of UC-Chinese joint ventures, *Journal of International Marketing*, 5 (3), 31-45.

Dwyer, F.R., Schurr, P.H. & Oh, S. (1987). Developing buyer-seller relationships. *Journal of Marketing*, 51, 11-27.

Dymza, W.A. (1988). Success and failures of joint ventures in developing countries: Lessons from experience. In F.J. Contractor & P. Lorange (Ed.) *Co-operative Strategies in International Business.* Lexington Books.

Faulkner, D. & Mcgee, J. (1995). Success and failure of international strategic alliances, *Evidence from In-Depth Case Studies*, (unpublished paper).

Franko, L.G. (1971). *Joint venture survival in Multinational Corporations*, New York: Praeger.

Garai, G. (1999) Leveraging the rewards of strategic alliances, *Journal of Business Strategy*, 20, 2, 40-43

Geringer, J.M. & Herbert, L. (1989). Control and performance of international joint ventures, *Journal of International Business Studies*, 20, 235-254.

Geringer, J.M. & Herbert, L. (1991). Measuring performance of international joint ventures. *Journal of International Business Studies*. 249-263.

Geyskens, J., Steenkamp, J.E.M., Scheer, L.K., & Kumar, N. (1996). The effects of trust and interdependence on relationship commitment: A transatlantic study, *International Journal of Research Marketing*, 303-17.

Glaister, K.W. & Buckley, P.J. (1994). UK international joint ventures: An analysis of patterns of activity and distribution, *British Journal of Management*, 5 (1), 35-51.

Glaister, K.W. and Wu, Wong (1994) Management and Performance of UK joint ventures in China, *Journal of Euromarketing*, 4,1,23-43

Glaister, K. and Buckley, P.J. (1996). Strategic motives for international alliance promotion. *Journal of Management Studies*, 33, 301-332.

Gomes-Casseres, B. (1987). Joint venture instability: Is it a problem? *Columbia Journal of World Business*, 22 (2), 97-107.

Good, L. (1972). United States joint ventures and manufacturing firms in Monterrey, Mexico: Comparative styles of management, *Unpublished Doctoral Dissertation*, Cornell University.

Habib, G.M. (1983). Conflict Measurement in the distribution channel of joint venture: An empirical investigation. *Unpublished Doctoral Dissertation*, Texas Tech University. Lubbock, Texas.

Hair, J.F., Anderson, R.E. Tatham, R.L & Black, W.C. (1998). *Multivariate Data Analysis*. New Jersey: Prentice Hall.

Hamel, G. (1991). Competition for competence and interpartner learning within international strategic alliances, *Strategic Management Journal*, 12, 83-103.

Harrigan, K.R. (1988). Joint ventures and competitive strategy, *Strategic Management Journal*, 12, 83-103.

Hennart, J.F. (1988). A transaction costs theory of equity joint ventures, *Strategic Management Journal*, 9, 4, 361-374.

Hergert, M. & Morris, D. (1988). Trends in international collaborative agreements, In F.J. Contractor & P. Lorange (Ed.) *Co-operative Strategies in International Business* (99-109). Lexington Books.

Holm, D.B., Eriksson, K. and Johanson, J. (1999). Creating vlaue through mutual commitment to business network relationships. *Strategic Management Journal*, 20, 5, 467-486.

Inkpen, A. (1998). Leraning and knowledge acquisition through international strategic alliances, *Academy of Management Executive*, 12, 4, 69-80.

Inkpen, A. and Li, K. (1999). Joint venture formation: Planning and knowledge gathering for success, *Organizational Dynamics*, 27, 4, 33-47.

Jain, C.S. (1987). Perspectives on international strategic alliances, *Advances in International Marketing*, 2, 103-20.

Johnson, J. (1999) Multiple commitments and conflicting loyalties in international joint venture management teams, *International Journal of Organizational Analysis*, 7,1, 54-71.

Kanter, R.M. (1988). The new alliances: How strategic partnerships are reshaping American Business, In H. Sawyer (Ed.) *Business in a Contemporary World*, New York: University Press of America.

Killing, J.P. (1983). *Strategies for joint venture success*, New York: Praeger.

Killing, J.P. (1988). Understanding alliances, the role of task and organizational complexity, In F.J. Contractor & P. Lorange (Ed.) *Co-operative Strategies in International Business* (55-67). Lexington Books.

Kogut, B. (1988). Joint ventures: Theoretical and empirical perspectives, *Strategic Management Journal*, 9 (4), 319-332.

Kumar, N. Scheer, L.K. & Steenkamp, J.E.M. (1995). The effects of perceived interdependence on dealer attitudes, *Journal of Marketing Research*, XXXII, 348-56.

Lane, H.W. & Beamish, P.W. (1990). Cross-cultural cooperative behavior in joint ventures in LDCs. *International Management Review*, 30, 87-102.

Lee, C. & Beamish, P.W. (1995). The characteristics and performance of Korean joint ventures in LDCs. *Journal of International Business Studies*. 26(3), 637-654.

Lin, Xiaohua and Germain, Richard (1998) Sustaining satisfactory joint venture relationships: The role of conflict resolution stategy, *Journal of International Business*, 29, 1, 179-196.

Lyles, M. A., Sulaiman, M., Barden, J. Q., Kechik, A. B. (1999) Factors affecting international joint venture performance: A study of Malaysian joint ventures, *Journal of Asian Business*, 15, 2, 1-20.

Mayer, R.C. Davies, J.H. & Schoorman, F.D. (1995). An integrative model of organizational trust, *Academy of Management Review*, 20 (3), 709-34.

McCutchen, W.W. Jr. and Swamidass, P.M (1998) Explaining the differences in domestic and cross boundary strategic alliances in the pharmaceutical and biotechnology industry, *International Journal of Technology Management*, 15, 3, 490-506.

Mjoen, H. & Tallman, S. (1997). Control and performance in international joint ventures, *Organization Science*, 8 (3), 257-74.

Mohr, J. & Nevin, J.R. (1990). Communication strategies in marketing channels: A theoretical perspective, *Journal of Marketing*, 54, 36-57.

Mohr, J. & Spekman, R. (1994). Characteristics of partnership success: Partnership attributes, communication behavior and conflict resolution techniques. *Strategic Management Journal*, 15, 135-52.

Monckza, R.M., Peterson, K.J., Handfield, R.B. & Ragatz, G.L. (1998). Success factors in strategic supplier alliances: The buying company perspective. *Decision Sciences*. 29 (3), 553-578.

Morgan, R.M. & Hunt, S.D. (1994). The commitment-trust theory of relationship marketing. *Journal of Marketing*, 58, 20-38.

Mowday, R.T., Porter, L.W. & Steers, R. (1982). *Employee-Organization linkages. The Psychology of Commitment, Absenteesism and Turnover*. New York: Academic Press.

Noordewier, T.G., John, G. & Nevin, J.R. (1990). Performance outcomes of purchasing arrangements in industrial buyer-vendor relationships, *Journal of Marketing*, 80-93.

Nunnally, J.C. (1978). *Psychometric Theory*, New York: McGraw Hill.

Ohmae, K. (1989). The global logic of strategic alliances, *Harvard Business Review*, Mar-Apr, 143-154.

Olson, L.B. & Singsuwan, K. (1997). The effect of partnership, communication and conflict resolution behavior on performance success of strategic alliances: American and Thai perspective. In Beamish, P.W. & Killing, J.P. (Ed.) *Cooperative strategies: Asian perspectives*. San Francisco, California: The New Lexington Press.

Parkhe, A. (1993). Messy research, methodological predispositions and theory development in international joint ventures, *Academy of Management Review*, 18 (2), 227-68.

Park, S. H. & Gerado, R.U. (1997). The effect of national culture, organizational complimentarity and economic motivation on joint venture dissolution, *Academy of Management Journal*, 40, 279-307.

Perlmutter, H.V. & Heenan, D.A. (1986). Co-operate to compete globally, *Harvard Business Review*, 136-150.

Pfeffer, J. & Salancik, G. (1978). *The external control of organizations.* New York: Harper.

Porter, M.E. & Fuller, M.B. (1986). Coalitions and global strategy, In Porter, M.E. (ed.) *Competition in Global Industries*, Boston: Harvard Business Press.

Pucik, V. (1988). Strategic alliances, organizational learning and competitive advantage: The HRM agenda, *Human Resource Management*, 27 (1), 77-93.

Renforth, W.E. (1974). A comparative study of joint international business ventures with family firm or non-family firm partners: The Caribbean community experience, Unpublished Doctoral Dissertation, Indiana University.

Reuer, J. (1998). The dynamics of effectiveness of international joint venture, *European Management Journal*, 16 (2), 160-68.

Reynolds, J.I. (1984). The pinched shoe effect of international joint ventures, *Columbia Journal of World Business*, 23-28.

Root, F.R. (1988). Some taxonomies of international co-operative arrangements, In F.J. Contractor & P. Lorange (Ed.) *Co-operative Strategies in International Business* (69-80). Lexington Books.

Salmond, D. & Spekman, H. (1986). Collaboration as a mode of managing long-term buyer-seller relationships.

Saxton, T. (1997). The effects of partner and relationship characteristics on alliance outcomes, *Academy of Management Journal*, 443-61.

Schaan, J.C. (1983). Parent control and joint venture success: The case of Mexico, *Unpublished Doctoral Dissertation*, University of Western Ontario. London, Ontario, Canada.

Shaw, V. and Kauser, S. (2000). The changing patterns of international strategic alliance activity by British firms, *Journal of General Management*, Summer (in print).

Spekman, R.E., Forbes, T.M. III, Isabella, L.A. and Macaroy, T.C. (1998), Alliance management: A review from the past and a look to the future, *Journal of Management Studies*, 35, 6, 747-772.

Terpstra, V. & Simonin, B.L. (1993). Strategic alliances in the triad: an exploratory study, *Journal of International Marketing*, 1 (1), 4-25.

Tilman, A.U. (1990). The influence of control and conflict on performance of Japanese-Thai joint ventures, *DBA Dissertation*, Nova University.

Tsang, E.W. K. (1999) A preliminary typology of learning in international strategic alliances, *Journal of World Business*, 34, 3, 211-229.

Vyas, N.M., Shelburn, W.L. and Rogers, D.C. (1995). An analysis of strategic alliances: Forms, functions and frameworks, *Journal of Business and Industrial Marketing*, 10, 3, 47-60.

Williams, J. D. and Han, S. and Qualls, W. J. (1998). A conceptual model and study of cross cultural business relationships, *Journal of Business Research*, 42, 2, 135-143.

Yoshino, M.Y. & Rangan, U.S. (1995). *Strategic alliances: An Entrepreneurial Approach to Globalization*, Boston: Harvard Business School Press.

Knowledge Transfer and Resource Sharing as Value Creation Mechanisms in Inbound Continental European Acquisitions

Richard Schoenberg

SUMMARY. Despite the growing popularity of acquisitions as a European market entry strategy, existing research reveals that many such acquisitions fail to generate positive shareholder returns. In an extension of the literature on operational synergy and value creation within acquisitions, this paper examines the types of knowledge transfer and resource sharing sought by inbound European acquirers together with their relative success rates. Data from 121 acquisitions into Continental Europe reveal that acquirers emphasize the attainment of operational synergy via knowledge transfer, particularly within the marketing and distribution functions. Disturbingly, however, the results also show that firms' ability to successfully transfer functional knowledge consistently falls short of their expectations, as does their ability to share resources within those activities that have a high local market knowledge content. These results are interpreted in the light of the recent knowledge-based literature and

---

Richard Schoenberg is Senior Lecturer in International Business Strategy, Imperial College Management School, University of London, 53 Prince's Gate, Exhibition Road, London SW7 2PG, United Kingdom (E-mail: r.schoenberg@ic.ac.uk).

[Haworth co-indexing entry note]: "Knowledge Transfer and Resource Sharing as Value Creation Mechanisms in Inbound Continental European Acquisitions." Schoenberg, Richard. Co-published simultaneously in *Journal of Euromarketing* (International Business Press, an imprint of The Haworth Press, Inc.) Vol. 10, No. 1, 2001, pp. 99-114; and: *Foreign Direct Investment and Strategic Alliances in Europe* (ed: Hong Liu) International Business Press, an imprint of The Haworth Press, Inc., 2001, pp. 99-114. Single or multiple copies of this article are available for a fee from The Haworth Document Delivery Service [1-800-342-9678, 9:00 a.m. - 5:00 p.m. (EST). E-mail address: getinfo@haworthpressinc.com].

implications for the value creation strategies of future European acquirers are outlined.

KEYWORDS. Cross-border acquisition, market entry, value creation, knowledge transfer, resource sharing

INTRODUCTION

Cross-border acquisitions are an increasingly popular form of European market entry. Data reveal that cross-border acquisitions have grown to represent 45% of the total annual expenditure on European mergers and acquisitions, which itself accounts for approximately one-third of global mergers and acquisitions activity. For example, 1998 alone saw the completion of 3,000 European cross-border acquisitions valued at over $220 billion (*Acquisitions Monthly*, February 1999). Prior research suggests that almost 70% of these acquisitions by number will have represented market entry transactions (Norburn and Schoenberg, 1994).

Acquirers face a major challenge to ensure that these acquisitions generate shareholder value. Although some researchers have reported that acquisitions into continental Europe create small positive abnormal returns for the shareholders of the acquiring firm (Markides and Oyon, 1998), others have found statistically significant evidence of negative shareholder wealth effects (Datta and Puia, 1995). Indeed, broader practitioner surveys reveal that 43% of cross-border acquisitions fail to produce a financial return in excess of the acquirer's cost of capital (Bleeke et al., 1993), while 45% fail to meet their initial strategic objectives (Rostand, 1994).

As one would expect given this mixed performance record a number of studies have investigated the antecedents of value creation within acquisitions. One research stream has focused on the link between economic performance and the strategic attributes of the combining firms, in particular the extent to which a target company's business should be related to that of the acquirer (see for example, Lubatkin, 1987; Seth, 1990). Yet although these studies have produced useful insights they have also been characterised by a lack of consensus (Flanagan, 1996).

In parallel, a related research stream has emerged which has attempted to identify a number of generic value creation mechanisms applicable to acquisitions. These researchers have converged on the central importance of operational synergy and present empirical evidence that the existence of opportunities to share resources or transfer knowledge results in improved acquisition performance (Brush, 1996; Capron and Pistre, 1999). However, we still know little regarding the relative ease of implementation of different types of knowledge transfer and resource sharing within cross-border acquisitions.

The current study therefore seeks to contribute to this emerging research stream by examining the types of knowledge transfer and resource sharing sought by acquirers into Europe together with their relative success rates. In particular we investigate the extent to which acquirers seek to transfer knowledge and share resources within seven functional and three administrative areas. We then establish for each functional and administrative area the degree to which the sought after operational synergies were actually achieved in practice. Thus the research identifies those business activities within which each type of operational synergy is most readily achieved and those within which European acquirers may expect significant implementation difficulty.

The remainder of the paper is structured as follows. The next section provides a more detailed review of the literature on value creation within acquisitions and argues towards the study's research question. The sample and methodology are then described and the results presented. The final sections discuss the results in the light of recent literature contributions and draw implications for practitioners.

VALUE CREATION WITHIN ACQUISITIONS

Early studies into value creation within acquisitions focused on the link between financial performance and the strategic attributes of the combining firms, in particular the extent to which a target company's business should be related to that of the acquirer. The foundation of these studies lay in the argument that the more closely related the two merging businesses are in terms of their products, markets and technologies, the greater the potential to create value by exploiting synergies based on economies of scale and scope and increased market power (Seth, 1990). However, the results of these studies have been less than conclusive. While some researchers confirmed that related acquisitions were associated with greater total wealth creation (Singh and Montgomery, 1987), others reported higher returns in unrelated acquisitions (Chatterjee, 1986), and others still concluded that there were no significant differences in the performance of the two types (Lubatkin, 1987; Seth, 1990).

This lack of consensus has been attributed in part to methodological issues within the studies (Seth, 1990). The classification of relatedness used in the studies, typically SIC codes or an external assessment of the product-markets served and technologies employed, at best provides only a crude measure of the ability to actually transfer value-creating capabilities between the companies post-acquisition (Nayyar, 1992). Later work attempts to overcome such limitations by employing more direct measures of strategic and resource relatedness. Yet, these authors, too, do not find conclusively that related acquisitions outperform unrelated ones (see for example, Markides and Williamson, 1996).

A second issue addressed within the "strategic fit" literature concerns the relationship between relative acquisition size and performance. These studies highlight that the acquisition of either a very small or a very large target company is associated with inferior financial performance (Kusewitt, 1985), but that outside of these circumstances the abnormal returns generated by a related acquisition generally rise with increasing relative acquisition size (Seth, 1990). These findings have been broadly confirmed in more recent work (Larsson and Finkelstein, 1999).

One criticism that has been levelled at the "strategic fit" studies reviewed above is that they tend to assume that *similarities* between the acquiring and acquired firms are the primary driver of potential value creation (Larsson and Finkelstein, 1999). Of course, *differences* between the two companies may also be a sound basis for value creation as the strengths of one company in a particular area complement the strengths of the other in a different area. The ability to create value through both similarities and differences within two merging organisations is recognised in a related research stream which has attempted to identify a number of generic value creation mechanisms applicable to acquisitions. Early contributions to this second research stream proposed four basic mechanisms of value creation applicable to acquisitions (Haspeslagh and Jemison, 1991; Porter, 1987):

1. *Resource Sharing*, in which certain operating assets of the two companies are combined and rationalized, leading to cost reductions through economies of scale or scope.

2. *Knowledge (skills) Transfer*, in which value-adding knowledge such as production technology, marketing know-how, or financial control skills are transferred from the acquiring firm to the acquired, or vice versa.
3. *Combination Benefits* where an increase in market power or a reduction in competitive intensity is achieved.
4. *Restructuring* where the acquired company contains undervalued or under-utilised assets. Here acquirers seek to exceed their acquisition costs by divesting certain assets at their true market value and by raising the productivity of the remaining assets.

More recent studies, however, have focused down on the central importance of operational synergy, which comprises both resource sharing and knowledge transfer, to value creation. Capron, Dussauge and Mitchell (1998) empirically argue that resource sharing and knowledge transfer are important even in those acquisitions where the principal motive may appear to be restructuring or the gaining of market power. These researchers found that operational synergy occurred no less frequently in acquisitions that resulted in price increases. Similarly, restructuring commonly involves extensive use of operational synergy, in the form of resource sharing and knowledge transfer, to gain productivity improvements in the target firm assets that are retained. This desire on the part of acquiring firms to exploit operational synergies has been attributed as a driving force behind the 1980s merger wave (Brush, 1996). Indeed, empirical evidence has also been forthcoming which confirms that the presence of such operational synergies are positively related to wealth creation for acquiring firm shareholders (Capron and Pistre, 1999) and long term improvements in the competitive positions of the both the acquiring and acquired companies (Brush, 1996; Capron, 1999).

Yet while these studies have provided detailed insights into the frequency and impacts of operational synergy, we still know little regarding the relative ease of implementation of different types of knowledge transfer and resource sharing within cross-border acquisitions. As Capron et al. (1998: 655) conclude, "It would also be fruitful to examine resource redeployment in international mergers and acquisitions in more detail...It would be useful to determine whether particular patterns of resource redeployment tend to associate with differential success."

Against this background the current paper explores the types of knowledge transfer and resource sharing sought by acquirers into Continental Europe together with their relative success rates. It addresses two principal research questions. First, to what extent do inbound European acquirers anticipate operational synergies and across which functional areas? Second, to what extent are the anticipated synergies actually realised in practice? In examining these questions the research seeks to extend our understanding of knowledge transfer and resource sharing as value creation mechanisms within European acquisitions.

METHODOLOGY

Data for the study were collected by postal questionnaire from 121 British cross-border acquisitions into Continental Europe as part of a wider research program into cross-border acquisitions (Schoenberg, 1997).

The questionnaire instrument was mailed to 239 British acquiring firms who were listed in the database of Acquisitions Monthly magazine as having completed a Continental European acquisition three to five years previously. The sample was comprised solely of related acquisitions as defined by two-digit SIC codes. Completed questionnaires were received from 131 of the firms, although subsequently 10 of the responses had to be discarded due to incomplete data. This left usable data from 121 acquisitions, representing a highly favourable response rate of 51%. Potential non-response bias within the sample was investigated by comparing respondents and non-respondents along the dimensions of relative acquisition size, country of acquisition and industry sector. Statistical tests revealed no evidence of bias.

The final sample of 121 acquisitions was comprised of British companies acquiring in a total of 8 Continental European nations, as detailed in Table 1. France (28% of sample), Germany (26%), Italy (13%), and the Netherlands (13%) were the most frequent destinations, a picture consistent with that of earlier studies of British cross-border acquisitions (Norburn and Schoenberg, 1994). The acquisitions also covered a relatively broad spread of industries, with manufacturing and service sectors making up 65% and 35% of the sample respectively. The most frequently represented industry sectors were distribution (12%), chemicals and pharmaceuticals (11%), financial services (10%), and mechanical engineering (9%).

In all cases respondents were current executive directors of the acquiring firm who had also been serving as directors at the time of the acquisition. The names and corporate addresses of the current acquiring firm directors were identified from the FAME database and as part of

TABLE 1. Target Nations of the Cross-Border Acquisitions

	Number	% of Sample
Belgium	6	5%
Denmark	3	3%
France	34	28%
Germany	32	26%
Italy	16	13%
Netherlands	16	13%
Portugal	1	1%
Spain	13	11%
Total	121	100%

the mail-out procedure these were compared with those listed in corporate directories for the year of the acquisition. This procedure ensured that questionnaires were mailed only to those directors who were in a position to be knowledgeable about the complete history of the acquisition.

The questionnaire captured data on the degree of knowledge transfer and resource sharing that acquirers sought and achieved between the two companies following the acquisition. Separate five-point Likert-type scales were developed to measure the degree of knowledge transfer and the degree of resource sharing along each of seven functional and three administrative activities (shown in Table 2 of the results section). The seven functional activities were adapted from Porter's (1985) value chain categories, while the three administrative activities were selected as those most frequently cited in Haspeslagh and Jemison's (1991) case-study descriptions of general management interdependence and are consistent with the definition of managerial capabilities adopted by Capron et al. (1998). In each case the scales ranged from (1) (no knowledge transfer/resource sharing) through (3) (some transfer/sharing) to (5) (significant transfer/sharing). The questionnaire rubric made clear that flows of knowledge transfer in either direction should be considered, i.e., from acquired to acquiring firm or vice-versa.

Respondents were first asked to state the extent to which each of the ten dimensions of knowledge transfer and resource sharing had been *actively sought as part of the original acquisition rationale*. Respondents were then requested to indicate the extent to which knowledge transfer and resource sharing *had actually been achieved* using the same set of items and scales. The timescale of the questionnaire survey (3-5 years following acquisition) meant that a minimum post-acquisi-

TABLE 2. Degree of Knowledge Transfer Sought and Achieved

	Knowledge Transfer Initially Sought			Knowledge Transfer Actually Achieved			Sought vs. Ach.
Business Activity	Mean	S.D.	% > 3	Mean	S.D.	% > 3	t-Stat
Research & Development	2.51	1.32	50%	2.33	1.18	45%	−2.44*
Product/Service Design	2.81	1.27	62%	2.47	1.09	48%	−4.25**
Purchasing/Supplier Relations	2.54	1.19	50%	2.36	1.07	44%	−2.48*
Service/Manufacturing Operations	2.81	1.21	62%	2.55	1.15	54%	−3.16**
Marketing & Sales	3.32	1.15	79%	2.89	1.09	63%	−4.70**
Distribution/Outlets	3.09	1.37	67%	2.77	1.27	61%	−3.72**
Customer Service	2.84	1.18	63%	2.59	1.11	57%	−3.61**
Strategic Planning	2.79	1.39	59%	2.45	1.17	54%	−3.64**
Financial Reporting	3.16	1.41	69%	3.01	1.31	67%	−1.45
Investment Appraisal	2.37	1.29	48%	2.29	1.20	46%	−1.02

Memo:
Mean and S.D.s are calculated from the responses to 5-point Likert type scales
"% > 3" indicates the percentage of acquirers seeking/achieving "some or more."
*p < 0.05; ** p < 0.01

tion integration period of 3 years had passed before the "actually achieved" data was collected. The selected timeframe is consistent with previous research which found that 80% of European cross-border acquirers expect to meet their acquisition objectives within 2½ years of completion of the purchase (Norburn and Schoenberg, 1994).

RESULTS

Table 2 shows the degree of knowledge transfer actively sought by inbound European acquirers within each of the ten functional and administrative activities, together with the levels actually achieved three to five years post-acquisition. Table 3 provides the same data for resource sharing by activity.

Initial inspection of the data reveals that acquirers into Europe emphasise the attainment of operational synergy via knowledge transfer. The percentage of acquirers seeking "some or more" knowledge transfer within any given functional or administrative area ranged from 48% to 79%, while the percentage seeking the same level of resource sharing varied between 41% and 64%. Further analysis (not shown) using a series of t-tests confirmed that knowledge transfer was sought to a statistically significant greater extent than resource sharing within seven out of the ten activities investigated. This result reinforces the increasingly recognised importance of the knowledge-based view of the

TABLE 3. Degree of Resource Sharing Sought and Achieved

Business Activity	Resource Sharing Initially Sought			Resource Sharing Actually Achieved			Sought vs. Ach.
	Mean	S.D.	% > 3	Mean	S.D.	% > 3	t-Stat
Research & Development	2.25	1.29	41%	2.16	1.27	39%	−1.21
Product/Service Design	2.38	1.25	45%	2.20	1.18	39%	−1.39*
Purchasing/Supplier Relations	2.37	1.38	46%	2.34	1.38	45%	−0.37
Service/Manufacturing Operations	2.29	1.35	41%	2.21	1.36	36%	−0.89
Marketing & Sales	2.96	1.42	64%	2.67	1.33	57%	−3.63**
Distribution/Outlets	2.64	1.50	50%	2.46	1.42	44%	−2.33*
Customer Service	2.57	1.52	51%	2.38	1.44	43%	−2.82**
Strategic Planning	2.44	1.49	46%	2.37	1.45	42%	−1.69
Financial Reporting	2.74	1.50	56%	2.72	1.50	53%	−0.40
Investment Appraisal	2.28	1.41	41%	2.20	1.33	39%	−1.47

Memo:
Mean and S.D.s are calculated from the responses to 5-point Likert type scales
"% > 3" indicates the percentage of acquirers seeking/achieving "some or more."
$^*p < 0.05$; $^{**}p < 0.01$

firm (Grant, 1996) and its relevance to acquisitions (Singh and Zollo, 1998).

In terms of individual areas of activity, acquirers particularly sought to gain both forms of operational synergy within their marketing, distribution and financial reporting activities. On average, 72% of acquirers sought "some or more" knowledge transfer within these three activities, while 57% sought the same degree of resource sharing. The lowest levels of knowledge transfer were pursued within the research and development, supply and investment appraisal activities. Resource sharing was also less common within the operations function itself. Overall, these findings suggest that the majority of acquirers into Europe attach primary importance to exploiting market based synergies whilst simultaneously securing financial control over their targets. This picture is consistent with more general research on European acquisitions which finds that the current wave of M&A activity in the region is motivated primarily by firms' desire to rapidly secure and build geographic market positions, rather than achieve the economies of scale that the architects of the 1992 Single European Market Programme predicted (Calori and Lubatkin, 1994).

Next a series of paired sample t-tests were conducted to compare the level of knowledge transfer and resource sharing initially sought with that actually achieved for each functional and administrative area. The results are shown in the final columns of Tables 2 and 3. Disturbingly, this analysis revealed relatively low levels of successful knowledge transfer. Acquirers failed to achieve their desired level of knowledge transfer within each of the seven functional areas and also within the strategic planning activity. For example, within the important marketing function while 79% of acquirers actively sought "some or more" knowledge transfer, only 63% attained this level. It was only in the areas of financial reporting and investment appraisal that the level of knowledge transfer achieved was not statistically different from that which was sought, although even in these areas the direction of the data was indicative of some difficulties of transfer. The results for resource sharing were somewhat more favourable. Anticipated levels of resource sharing were almost achieved within the research and development, supply, operations and administrative activities. However, statistically significant shortfalls were evident in the design, marketing, distribution and customer service functions.

DISCUSSION

The major finding of this study is that while inbound European acquirers emphasise the attainment of operational synergy via knowledge transfer, their ability to successfully transfer functional knowledge consistently falls short of their expectations. The issue of knowledge management has received considerable attention in the academic literature (see for example Grant, 1996) and recent research serves to highlight possible factors that may be constraining the implementation of knowledge transfer within cross-border acquisitions. Szulanski (1996) has established empirically that there are three principal barriers to internal knowledge transfer within an organisation: a lack of absorptive capacity on behalf of the recipient, an arduous relationship between the source of the knowledge and the recipient, and causal ambiguity regarding the exact nature of the knowledge to be transferred. Each of these barriers may be present within an inbound European acquisition.

The profile of the typical Continental European target company may in certain circumstances raise questions as to the firm's capacity for absorbing substantive functional know-how transferred from a much larger acquiring company. An analysis of this study's sample revealed that two-thirds of the target firms were owner-managed businesses with a turnover of under 15 million ECU prior to acquisition, a profile that is fully consistent with other surveys of European acquisitions (Norburn and Schoenberg, 1994; Angwin and Savill, 1997). Furthermore, of the owner-managed businesses over 60% had been in operation for only 25 years or less with the implication that the original entrepreneur may still have been in position at the time of acquisition. These data suggest that a high proportion of acquired European companies may be at an early position within their corporate lifecycles and therefore perhaps without the necessary corporate systems, structures and managerial resources to facilitate the absorption of specialist functional knowledge (Norburn, Manning and Birley, 1986).

The second impediment to knowledge transfer, the existence of an arduous relationship between the source of the knowledge and the recipient, may be particularly pertinent within an acquisition context (Dussauge and Garrette, 1999). Research on domestic acquisitions has highlighted that differences in organisational culture and managerial approach between the two combining firms can result in feelings of uncertainty, insecurity and alienation amongst acquired firm employees, which in severe cases can lead to disruptive behaviours and acts of rejection and non-compliance (Elsass and Veiga, 1994; Nahavandi and Malekzadeh, 1994). Thus, in many cases an acquisition in itself may generate arduous relationships which are not conducive to knowledge transfer. These issues may be compounded for inbound European acquirers by the cross-border nature of their transactions. In addition to possible differences in organisational culture, cross-border acquisitions involve the combination of personnel and capabilities that may be characterised by differences in language (Olie, 1994), national culture (Morosini, Shane, and Singh, 1998) and institutional and social contexts (Olie, 1994). Previous studies on cross-border partnerships have shown that such cross-national differences can lead to heightened miscommunication and misunderstandings (Lane and Beamish, 1990; Schoenberg, Denuelle and Norburn, 1995), which may further impede the creation of the positive relationships necessary for effective knowledge transfer.

Finally, the cross-border nature of inbound European acquisitions may also increase causal ambiguity regarding the exact nature of the knowledge which the acquirer seeks to transfer. Differences in national cultural and institutional contexts may create ambiguity surrounding the precise knowledge elements that lie behind functional capability in a given geographic market. Managers' repertoires and routines vary from one nation to another and what works in one nation may not be readily translated by those from others (Newman and Nollen, 1996). For example, acquirers from "low context" Anglo-Saxon cultures may have difficulty in identifying the key role played by deeply rooted personal networks spanning customers and suppliers when acquiring a target company from a "higher context" culture such as Italy (Hall, 1977; Porter, 1990). This line of argument is supported by research from the international management field that finds that different national cultures adopt different managerial approaches and practices within functional areas including product development (Nakata and Sivakumar, 1996), human resource management (Luthans, Welsh and Rosenkrantz, 1993) and strategic planning (Schneider and De Meyer, 1991).

In summary, the finding that inbound European acquirers consistently fail to achieve their desired levels of knowledge transfer can be interpreted in the light of the recent knowledge based literature. The above section has argued that each of three established barriers to organisational knowledge transfer may be heightened within the context of a cross-border acquisition into Europe.

Another interesting finding of this study concerns the inter-functional variance seen with regard to the implementation of resource sharing. Whilst the sought after levels of resource sharing were almost achieved within the research and development, supply, operations and administrative activities, significant shortfalls were evident in the design, marketing, distribution and customer service functions. It has been argued that each of these latter functions require a degree of local market knowledge for their successful conduct (Calori and Lawrence, 1991; Whitelock and Pimblett, 1997). Resource sharing within these "market-orientated" functions therefore may be impeded by the same cross-national knowledge transfer issues highlighted above, namely the presence of causal ambiguity and arduous relationships. The implementation of a common product design function across bidder and target, for example, could be constrained by the existence of subtle local consumer preferences and/or conflicts over the manner in which the design process is managed arising from different national preferences (Nakata and Sivakumar, 1996).

A key implication for practitioners that arises out of these arguments is that the existence of arduous relationships or causal ambiguity within a European acquisition may reduce its ability to successfully create value through the transfer of knowledge or the sharing of resources. The presence of any ambiguity regarding the precise source of a desired functional capability suggests that an initial challenge for acquirers is to correctly recognise and codify the exact knowledge elements that must be transferred or shared in order to replicate the capability. Indeed, other recent acquisitions research has shown that the ability to codify knowledge is associated with superior performance even in domestic acquisitions which wish to achieve high levels of integration (Zollo and

Singh, 1998). As has been argued above, the presence of causal ambiguity generated by a cross-border context is likely to add further complexity to the knowledge codification process, thereby further hindering the successful replication of any given capability.

Furthermore, knowledge, particularly tacit knowledge, is frequently embedded in specific individuals within an organisation and its transfer between the bidder and target or vice-versa may require a personal exchange between the knowledge holder and the recipient (Szulanski, 1996). This suggests two further challenges for the acquirer. First, can the specific individual "knowledge holders" and appropriate recipients be identified and brought together? Second, can an atmosphere conducive to forming positive relationships be created that will facilitate such personal exchanges?

These challenges, in turn, reinforce the need for detailed pre-bid implementation planning. At the macro level, commercial and organisational due diligence may serve to highlight areas of potential causal ambiguity and arduous relationships. Commercial due diligence should provide in-depth analyses of the target company's national, market and customer characteristics and highlight any contextual differences from the acquirer's domestic environment, while organisational due diligence serves to assess the compatibility of organisational cultures and management styles. At the micro level, acquirers need to be satisfied at the pre-bid stage that key value creating knowledge elements can either be codified or that the individual "knowledge holders" can be identified and physical arrangements, often secondments, made to allow the necessary personal exchanges.

CONCLUSIONS

Overall, this study provides empirical evidence that cross-border acquirers consistently underestimate the difficulty in implementing planned operational synergies and gives a further insight into why inbound European acquisitions continue to generate disappointing shareholder returns. In particular, the ability to transfer functional knowledge appears to fall short of most acquirers expectations as does the ability to share market-orientated resources. At one level these results suggest that acquirers whose value creation strategies emphasise the sharing of non-market orientated resources, such as R&D, production or administrative facilities, may enjoy greater success than those that rely on other forms of operational synergy. More fundamentally, however, they indicate that acquirers into Europe must place greater emphasis on detailed pre-bid implementation planning if value is to be successfully created by the transfer of market orientated knowledge which frequently serves as the prime motivation for such acquisitions. This implementation planning should focus particularly on establishing the extent to which codification of the knowledge is possible and whether managerial relationships conducive to its effective transfer can be created.

REFERENCES

Angwin, D. & Savill, B. (1997). Strategic Perspectives on European Cross-Border Acquisitions: A View From Top European Executives. *European Management Journal*, 15 (4), 423-435.

Bleeke, J., Isono, J., Ernst, D., & Weinburg, D. (1993). Succeeding at Cross-Border M&A. In Bleeke, J. & Ernst, D. (Eds.), *Collaborating to Compete: Using Strategic Alliances and Acquisitions in the Global Marketplace* (pp79-90). New York: J. Wiley & Sons.

Brush, T. (1996). Predicted Change in Operational Synergy and Post-Acquisition Performance of Acquired Businesses. *Strategic Management Journal*, 17 (1), 1-24.

Calori, R. & Lawrence, P. (Eds.) (1991). *The Business of Europe.* London: Sage Publications.

Calori, R. & Lubatkin, M. (1994). Euro Mergers 1993: Viewpoints and Predictions. In von Krogh, G., Sinatra, A., & Singh, H. (Eds.). *The Management of Corporate Acquisitions* (pp128-143). London: Macmillan.

Capron, L. (1999). The Long Term Performance of Horizontal Acquisitions. *Strategic Management Journal*, 20 (11), 987-1018.

Capron, L., Dussauge, P., & Mitchell, W. (1998). Resource Redeployment Following Horizontal Acquisitions in Europe and North America 1988-1992. *Strategic Management Journal*, 19 (7), 631-661.

Capron, L. & Pistre, N. (1999). *Exploring the Variations in Stock Returns of Acquiring Firms Involved in Horizontal Acquisitions.* Paper presented at 19th Annual International Conference of the Strategic Management Society, Berlin, Germany.

Chatterjee, S. (1986). Type of Synergy and Economic Value: The Impact of Acquisitions on Merging and Rival Firms. *Strategic Management Journal*, 7 (2), 119-139.

Datta, D. & Puia, G. (1995). Cross-Border Acquisitions: An Examination of the Influence of Relatedness and Cultural Fit on Shareholder Value Creation in US Acquiring Firms. *Management International Review*, 35 (4), 337-359.

Dussauge, P. & Garrette, B. (1999). *Cooperative Strategy: Competing Successfully through Strategic Alliances*. Chichester: J. Wiley & Sons.

Elsass, P. & Veiga, J. (1994). Acculturation in Acquired Organisations: A Force-Field Perspective. *Human Relations*, 47 (4), 431-453.

Flanagan, D. (1996). Announcements of Purely Related and Purely Unrelated Mergers and Shareholder Returns: Reconciling the Relatedness Paradox. *Journal of Management*, 22 (6), 823-835.

Grant, R. (1996). Toward a Knowledge-Based Theory of the Firm. *Strategic Management Journal*, 17 (Winter Special Issue), 109-122.

Hall, E. (1977). *Beyond Culture.* New York: Doubleday.

Haspeslagh, P. & Jemison, D. (1991). *Managing Acquisitions.* New York: Free Press.

Healy, P., Palepu, K. and Ruback, R. (1997). Which Takeovers Are Profitable? Strategic or Financial? *Sloan Management Review*, 38 (4), 45-57.

Kusewitt, J. (1985). An Exploratory Study of Strategic Acquisition Factors Relating to Performance. *Strategic Management Journal*, 6 (2), 151-169.

Lane, H. & Beamish, P. (1990). Cross-Cultural Cooperative Behaviour in Joint Ventures in LDCs. *Management International Review*, 30 (1), 87-102.

Larsson, R. and Finkelstein, S. (1999). Integrating Strategic, Organisational, and Human Resource Perspectives on Mergers and Acquisitions: A Case Survey of Synergy Realization, *Organization Science*, 10 (1), 1- 26.

Lubatkin, M. (1987). Merger Strategies and Stockholder Value. *Strategic Management Journal*, 8 (1), 39-53.

Luthans, F., Welsh, D., & Rosenkrantz, S. (1993). What do Russian Managers Really Do? An Observational Study with Comparisons to US Managers. *Journal of International Business Studies*, 24 (4), 741-761.

Markides, C. & Oyon, D. (1998). International Acquisitions: Do They Create Value for Shareholders? *European Management Journal*, 16 (2), 125-135.

Markides, C. & Williamson, P. (1996). Corporate Diversification and Organisational Structure: A Resource Based View. *Academy of Management Journal*, 39 (2), 340-367.

Morosini, P., Shane, S. & Singh, H. (1998). National Cultural Distance and Cross-Border Acquisition Performance. *Journal of International Business Studies*, 29 (1), 137-158.

Nahavandi, A, & Malekzadeh, A. (1994). Successful Mergers Through Acculturation. In von Krogh, G., Sinatra, A., & Singh, H. (Eds.) *The Management of Corporate Acquisitions* (pp. 293-306). London: Macmillan.

Nakata, C. & Sivakumar, K. (1996). National Culture and New Product Development: An Integrative Review. *Journal of Marketing*, 60 (1), 61-72.

Nayyar, P. (1992). On The Measurement of Corporate Diversification Strategy: Evidence From Large US Service Firms. *Strategic Management Journal*, 13 (3), 219-235.

Newman, K. & Nollen, S. (1996). Culture and Congruence: The Fit Between Management Practices and National Culture. *Journal of International Business Studies*, 27 (4), 753-779.

Norburn, D., Manning K., & Birley, S. (1986). Beyond Intrapreneurship: The Metamorphosis of Larger Corporations. *Leadership and Organisational Development Journal*, 7 (3), 21-26.

Norburn, D. & Schoenberg, R. (1994). European Cross-Border Acquisition: How Was It for You? *Long Range Planning*, 27 (4), 25-34.

Olie, R. (1990). Culture and Integration Problems in International Mergers and Acquisitions. *European Management Journal*, 8 (2), 206-215.

Olie, R. (1994). Shades of Culture and Institutions in International Mergers. *Organisation Studies*, 15 (3), 381-405.

Porter, M. (1985). *Competitive Advantage: Creating and Sustaining Superior Performance*. New York: Free Press.

Porter, M. (1987). From Competitive Advantage to Corporate Strategy. *Harvard Business Review*, 65 (3), 43-59.

Porter, M. (1990). *The Competitive Advantage of Nations*, New York: Free Press.

Rostand, A. (1994). *Optimizing Managerial Decisions during the Acquisition Integration Process*. Paper presented at 14th Annual Strategic Management Society International Conference, Paris, France.

Schoenberg, R. (1997). *The Impact of Management Style Differences on the Performance of European Cross-Border Acquisitions*. Unpublished Doctoral Dissertation, University of London.

Schoenberg, R., Denuelle, N., & Norburn, D. (1995). National Conflict within European Alliances, *European Business Journal*, 7 (1), 8-16.

Schneider, S. & De Meyer, A. (1991). Interpreting and Responding to Strategic Issues: The Impact of National Culture. *Strategic Management Journal*, 12 (4), 307-320.

Seth, A. (1990). Value Creation in Acquisitions: A Re-Examination of Performance Issues. *Strategic Management Journal*, 11 (2), 99-116.

Singh, H. & Montgomery, C. (1987). Corporate Acquisition Strategies and Economic Performance. *Strategic Management Journal*, 8 (4), 377-386.

Singh, H. & Zollo, M. (1998). *The Impact of Knowledge Codification, Experience Trajectories and Integration Strategies on the Performance of Corporate Acquisitions*. Paper presented at 18th Annual International Conference of the Strategic Management Society, Orlando, USA.

Szulanski, G. (1996). Exploring Internal Stickiness: Impediments to the Transfer of Best Practice within the Firm. *Strategic Management Journal*, 17 (Winter Special Issue), 27-43.

Whitelock, J. & Pimblett, C. (1997). "The Standardization Debate in International Marketing," *Journal of Global Marketing*, 10 (3), 45-66.

Index

In this index, page numbers in *italic* designate figures; page numbers followed by the letter "t" designate tables.

For Product Safety Concerns and Information please contact our EU representative GPSR@taylorandfrancis.com
Taylor & Francis Verlag GmbH, Kaufingerstraße 24, 80331 München, Germany

www.ingramcontent.com/pod-product-compliance
Lightning Source LLC
LaVergne TN
LVHW020629300926
849161LV00004B/651

9780789016522